I0459177

# ROMANS:

## DISPENSATIONALLY CONSIDERED

---

## VOLUME 1 OF 2

---

### A GRACE EXPOSITIONAL COMMENTARY

#### SECOND EDITION

## Steven L. Tackett

Compiled and edited by:
## Dr. David Alan Greene

GRACEWORD PUBLISHING

# Contents

To my parents, Buster and Erma Tackett

Study to shew thyself approved unto God,
a workman that needeth not to be ashamed,
*rightly dividing* the word of truth.

– The Apostle Paul

# Acknowledgements

In the writing of this book, I would like to express my deep gratitude to my beloved wife Stephanie. She has been a constant source of support and encouragement. A special thanks to my brother Dave Greene. He used my lectures on Romans to compile and edit this book. I would also like to thank Frances Greene who, through her generosity, provided the financial means by which this book was originally published.

It is my hope and prayer that this book will bring many to a deeper understanding of Scripture . . . *rightly divided.*

# Preface

There may be some who are unfamiliar with the expository style of Bible teaching. It is an incredible *tool* to help us learn, understand, and enjoy our Bible. Many have never heard the word *dispensation* before even though Paul uses this word repeatedly in his epistles. I assure you that Dispensational Theology is *not* a new theology or sect or religion. In fact, Paul instructed his apprentice in the faith, Timothy, to follow this instruction for correct interpretation. 2 Timothy 2:15:

> 15 **Study to shew thyself approved unto God, a workman that needeth not to be ashamed, <u>rightly dividing</u> the word of truth**

He told Timothy to study a certain way so that he would not be embarrassed or ashamed by incorrectly interpreting God's Word. The Greek word which is interpreted in the KJB as *rightly dividing* is *orthotomeo*. It is a compound word. The first part is *ortho* like the words *orthodox* and *orthopedic*. *Ortho* means *precisely, exactly,* or *correctly.* The second part of this Greek word is *tomeo.* We find it at the end of words like mastec*tomy* and tonsillec*tomy.* The Greek word *ex* means out. If we put this together, the meaning is revealed. A tonsillectomy is carefully cutting out the tonsil. This may seem like a lot of work to make a point, but this is very important. Let us put the word together: *ortho* + *tomeo* literally means to *carefully cut* or *cut with great precision.* The KJB translates the word as "rightly divide." Some newer versions translate it "correctly handles," "correctly explains," or "accurately handling." By doing so, they completely miss Paul's point. We are to carefully and with great precision "cut" or "divide" the Bible in order to correctly interpret it.

Dispensational thought is a tool. What makes this unique? There are three characteristics that are the hallmark of the dispensational approach to interpreting God's Word. They are: (1) literal, (2) historical, and (3) grammatical. However, what is most important, is the concept of dividing or cutting the Bible into different sections called *dispensations* which means *administrations.*

God chose to use these *dispensations* in His plan to restore Creation. When examining Scripture, it is critical not to read into the Scripture our own thoughts or ideas. We must allow Scripture to speak for itself. When we use the *literal-grammatical-historical* approach, we need to look at who is speaking, to whom it is speaking, what is being said, and the context in which it was written. The Bible was written by God through the Holy Spirit. It is His message or special revelation. This message is something God wants the reader to understand. It is not some complicated or cryptic message that only God's elite can explain. As such, it is our goal to understand the important message intended for us in Paul's letter to the Romans. In this book I use the King James Bible (KJB) because I feel it is the only English version that is faithful to the Textus Majorus or original text.

Paul wrote letters, called *epistles*, to both Timothy and Titus with instructions on the proper handling of God's Word in their ministry. We have already examined it once regarding the specific word for *rightly dividing*, but let us look at it again. 2 Timothy 2:15:

> 15 **Study to shew thyself approved unto God, a workman that needeth not to be ashamed, rightly dividing <u>the word of truth.</u>**

Paul refers to the Bible as the *Word of Truth*. We must

agree on this. Otherwise, these words carry no weight or authority. He writes to Timothy concerning the importance of Scripture. 2 Timothy 3:16–17:

> **16 All scripture is given by inspiration of God, and is profitable for doctrine, for reproof, for correction, for instruction in righteousness: 17 That the man of God may be perfect, thoroughly furnished unto all good works**

Paul tells Timothy that all Scripture is profitable for *doctrine* which means *teaching*. The goal is that the man of God may be complete in his understanding and thoroughly prepared to do good works. This includes the ability to apply the Word of Truth and teach it.

What would be an example of *rightly dividing* the Word of Truth? To start with, we can see that the Bible is divided into two testaments. I think we would all agree that there is a difference between the Old Testament and the New Testament, yet both are the Word of Truth. They are both true. However, the Old Testament does not apply to us today in the same way that portions of the New Testament do. This is another example of right division in Scripture. There is a division which is even greater. It is the division between *prophecy* and *mystery*.

Prophecy can be seen throughout the Old Testament. The other, called Mystery, is not as well-known because it is not taught. Look at Ephesians 3:1–5:

> 1 **For this cause I Paul, the prisoner of Jesus Christ for you Gentiles, 2 If ye have heard of the dispensation of the grace of God which is given me to you-ward: 3 <u>How that by revelation he made known unto me the mystery</u>; (as I wrote afore in few words, 4 Whereby, when ye read, ye may understand my knowledge in the mystery of Christ) 5 <u>Which in other ages was not made known</u> unto the sons of men, as it is now revealed unto his holy apostles and prophets by the Spirit;**

We can see that the Lord Jesus Christ gave the Apostle Paul the revelation of the *mystery*. Here the word *mystery* does not mean something that is not understandable or mystic. It means something that had not yet been revealed. This *mystery* had been hidden in the past and now is made known. Notice he refers to *the dispensation of the grace of God*. There is the word *dispensation!* The Lord Jesus Christ revealed to Paul this *mystery* for a purpose. What was that purpose?

Let us carefully consider the words Paul used, "which is given me to you-ward: how that by revelation he made known unto me the mystery" (vv. 2–3). It was given to Paul who would then give it to us. Paul often refers to himself as the Apostle to the Gentiles and as a prisoner of Jesus Christ for us Gentiles. He is constrained to the task which the Lord Jesus Christ gave him. The last verse above would be understood to mean that God revealed to Paul something that He had not revealed to any man before. This book will examine Romans in view of these two major divisions or distinctions in Scripture. That is the *prophecy* given to Israel by its prophets and the *revelation of the mystery* given to Paul for the Gentiles.

To get a better understanding as to what the major differences between the *prophecy program* and the *mystery program*, I will give examples. The *prophecy program* is centered around Israel. There are several promises or prophecies in the Old Testament all of which are made to Israel. Remember, the Church, called the Body of Christ, does not exist until the New Testament. This prophecy concerns an earthly kingdom which will be established forever. 2 Samuel 7:10:

10 **Moreover I will appoint a place for my people Israel, and will plant them, that they may dwell in a place of their**

**own, and move no more; neither shall
the children of wickedness afflict them
any more, as beforetime,**

Ask yourself this question: "About whom is this
verse speaking?" It should be clear that it is about Israel. The prophet Nathan delivers this message from
God to King David. Verse 11:

11 **And as since the time that I com-
manded judges to be over my people Israel, and have caused thee to rest from
all thine enemies. Also the LORD
telleth thee that he will make thee an
house.**

The above verses speak about Israel and God's
desire to give them rest from their enemies. How will
God accomplish this? Verses 12–13:

12 **And when thy days be fulfilled, and
thou shalt sleep with thy fathers, I will
set up thy seed after thee, which shall
proceed out of thy bowels, and I will establish his kingdom.** 13 **He shall build
an house for my name, and I will stab-
lish the throne of his kingdom for ever.**

The first verse in the Gospel of Matthew says, "The

book of the generation of Jesus Christ, the son of David, the son of Abraham" (Matt. 1:1). Notice that Jesus Christ is the direct descendent of King David. Matthew 1:16–17:

> 16 And thine house and thy kingdom shall be established for ever before thee: thy throne shall be established for ever. 17 According to all these words, and according to all this vision, so did Nathan speak unto David.

If we read the Scripture here in context, it would be difficult for us to apply this promise to anyone other than Israel. We read in the prophet Daniel 2:44:

> 44 And in the days of these kings shall the God of heaven set up a kingdom, which shall never be destroyed: and the kingdom shall not be left to other people, but it shall break in pieces and consume all these kingdoms, and it shall stand for ever.

In the Gospel of Matthew, the Lord instructs His disciples to pray in this manner. Matthew 6:10:

> 10 Thy kingdom come. Thy will be done in earth, as it is in heaven.

The Lord Jesus Christ instructs his disciples to pray for the Kingdom to come to Earth because it was promised to them, Israel, in prophecy. If we examine each of the other promises or prophecies made in the Old Testament, we can confirm that they were also made to Israel.

Now, let us compare the above to what the Apostle Paul teaches according to the revelation of *the mystery* in the Dispensation of Grace. That would be about us, the Church — the Body of Christ. He teaches that the Body of Christ is a living organism; not a Kingdom. Speaking to the Gentiles, Paul concludes with the following statement. 1 Corinthians 12:27:

> 27 **Now ye are the body of Christ, and members in particular.**

Earlier in this same chapter, Paul explained the Body of Christ. Verses 12–14:

> 12 **For as the body is one, and hath many members, and all the members of that one body, being many, are one body: so also is Christ. 13 For by one Spirit are we all baptized into one body, whether we be Jews or Gentiles, whether we be bond or free; and have been all made to**

**drink into one Spirit. 14 For the body is not one member, but many.**

So, the Body of Christ is a different entity than that of the Kingdom. This may be difficult for some who have never heard of rightly dividing the Scriptures. The preceding example should be sufficient for us to continue with our examination of the facts; carefully considering them literally, historically, and grammatically.

My friend, if we believe the gospel as Paul outlines it in 1 Corinthians, then we are already a member of the Body of Christ. Here is the Gospel of Grace in a nutshell. 1 Corinthians 15:1–4:

**1 Moreover, brethren, I declare unto you the gospel which I preached unto you, which also ye have received, and wherein ye stand; 2 By which also ye are saved, if ye keep in memory what I preached unto you, unless ye have believed in vain. 3 For I delivered unto you first of all that which I also received, how that [1] Christ died for our sins according to the scriptures; 4 And [2] that he was buried, and [3] that he rose again the third day according to the scriptures:**

Notice that Paul uses the definite article and not the indefinite article. He says *the* gospel and not *a* gospel. Accepting this gospel, we are immediately saved and a member of the Church—the Body of Christ. We are not looking forward to a Kingdom that is a future promise. That promise was made to Israel. During this current Dispensation of Grace, we have a choice. We can either believe in what Christ has already done for us or we can reject it. Christ has completed everything necessary for our salvation. Everything Believing what Christ has already done is the key to salvation in the Dispensation of Grace. We are saved by God Who gave up His Son for us. Christ died on the Cross, was buried, and was resurrected according to the Scriptures. This paid the penalty of our sins—past, present, and future—in full. One might ask, "Is this all we need to do to be saved?" Look at Ephesians 2:4–7:

> 4 But God, who is rich in mercy, for his great love wherewith he loved us, 5 Even when we were dead in sins, hath quickened  us [made us alive] together with Christ, (by grace ye are saved;) 6 And hath raised us up together, and made us sit together in heavenly places in Christ Jesus: 7 That in the ages to come he might shew the exceeding riches of his grace in his kindness to

**ward us through Christ Jesus.**

The next two verses are critical to understanding the extent of Christ's work for us. Verses 8–9:

8 **For by grace are ye saved through faith; and that not of yourselves: it is the gift of God:** 9 **Not of works, lest any man should boast.**

Spiritually, we are seated with Christ in the heavenly places, not waiting on earth for the promised Kingdom. Note the last verse states that we are saved by *grace*, a gift, through *faith*, believing what Christ has done on our behalf. There is nothing we can do; nothing that we can add to what Christ has already done. Think about this for a moment.

Many Christians who have been taught in the various denominational divisions may feel uncomfortable with this statement. Many feel they need to do something to maintain that salvation. Ask yourself the following questions. Does anyone need to pay for a gift? Is a gift not free? Does anyone need to work or do something to earn a gift? If they do, then it is not a gift. It is either wages or some other form of exchange, but it would not be a gift because a gift is free!

The benefit of Romans is that it is a foundational book. God presents His plan before all the world so that everyone can see. We will see that God is justified in His eternal plans and He is worthy to be glorified. It is my desire to walk you through Paul's wonderful book, verse by verse. I want you to understand what the words say, not what I say or what you have been taught. We are comfortable knowing what we are taught. We trust our teachers and believe what they say. However, if you had a different teacher, would you believe something different? Who would be right? What is truth? Paul answers this question. Here it is for the third time. 2 Timothy 2:15:

> 15 **Study to shew thyself approved unto God, a workman that needeth not to be ashamed, rightly dividing <u>the word of truth</u>.**

Our goal is to get it right so that when we stand before God, we will not be ashamed or embarrassed. The Bible is the Word of Truth!

The basis of our doctrine must be the Bible. There are numerous ways to interpret the Bible. Which way is correct? Remember that Scripture is inspired by God. Therefore, Scripture is to interpret Scripture. We must test what we are taught. In contracts, there is usually a provision that states if there is a portion of the contract in error, the entire contract would not become null and void, but, rather, only that specific portion. The Bible does not have that luxury. It is either all true or it is not. Paul gives us an example as to how teaching on Scripture should be handled. He showed up in Berea and started teaching. Many of the Bereans had never met him before. How did they know what Paul was teaching was correct? He writes about these noble Bereans. Acts 17:11:

> 11 **These were more noble than those in Thessalonica, in that they received the word with all readiness of mind, and searched the scriptures daily, whether those things were so.**

Our answer is to use Scripture to support Scripture. These are called proof texts. It is the way we support our doctrinal positions. This is the concept that we will apply in this book. Not only will you learn what Paul is teaching in the Book of Romans, but, for many of you, it will be the first time you see how correct doctrine is supported by Scripture. Correct doctrine must be in agreement with Scripture as a whole. Taking Scripture out of context is a big no-no since it allows people to twist God's Word.

Since Romans is the first Pauline epistle in the New Testament, it provides the basis upon which all of his other letters which follow are to be interpreted. It is my prayer that the study of Romans increases your knowledge and confidence in your faith. If you are unfamiliar with this book, you have many wonderful truths to discover. Carefully consider what is being taught, all the while comparing Scripture to Scripture, and you will understand the riches of His Word. With that, I will end with the closing words to Paul's letter to the believers in Rome. Romans 16:25–27:

> 25 **Now to him that is of power to stablish you according to my gospel, and the preaching of Jesus Christ, according to the revelation of the mystery, which was kept secret since the world began,** 26 **But now is made manifest, and by the scriptures of the prophets, according to the commandment of the everlasting God, made known to all nations for the obedience of faith:** 27 **To God only wise, be glory through Jesus Christ for ever. Amen.**

# Introduction

Let us start with a brief overview of Romans. Understanding the overall structure of the book will allow us to appreciate the author's intention and purpose. The main theme of Romans is the unrighteousness of man and the righteousness of God; the hopelessness of man and the hope of God revealed. The entire book is doctrinally based. It lays out an argument like an attorney speaking before a jury making his case. We can break down the book of Romans into three sections.

The first eight chapters concern the issues of sin, salvation, sanctification, and eternal security of the believer. In Romans 1, we see in Paul's greeting and salutation that he states the purpose and theme of the entire letter. In verses 16 and 17, in particular, he says, "I am not ashamed of the gospel of Christ: for it is the power of God unto salvation to everyone that believeth." In chapters 1 through 3, Paul presents the issue of sin and the righteous judgment of God. The indictment of man applies to both Jew and non-Jew alike. It concludes that all mankind is without excuse before God. Furthermore, it presents the fact that mankind is helpless to satisfactorily regain righteousness before God. Therefore, all are guilty before God. There is none who are righteous; no not one.

In chapters 3 through 5, we get into the doctrine of salvation by faith in Christ's work alone. Justification is being made through His blood. In chapters 6 through 8, we will learn the doctrine of sanctification. There we will understand the fact that we are dead to sin, and the way we are to live as believers is by walking according to the Spirit of God. Chapter 8 devotes time to understanding the security of the believer and the believer's ultimate glorification. In fact, those who believe the Gospel of Grace are joint-heirs with Christ. They will be glorified with Him and from Him there will be no separation. A key Pauline doctrine is that, positionally, believers are safe *in Christ*. They cannot be separated from Him. They are eternal secure. All of this is available to all who choose to believe.

Chapters 9 through 11 look at the present position of Israel, God's Chosen People, in this current Dispensation of Grace. God is not finished with His people. God Himself will fulfill the promises and covenants He made with them. Paul looks at the temporary suspension of Israel's Kingdom Promises, the present offer for them to participate in the offer of grace, and their prophetic future. Chapter 9 deals with Israel's past and God's purpose for the elect in Israel. We learn that not everyone who is a Jew will be saved; only those who believe. The fact that Israel rejected their Messiah allowed for an opportunity for the Gentiles to receive mercy. Being ignorant of God's righteousness, Israel goes about establishing their own righteousness according to the Law. They stumbled in unbelief when the Messiah came to them and they became a disobedient people. In Chapter 11, we see Israel's future. Even though Israel had rejected their Messiah, they will, in the future, receive salvation through Christ. This will happen when all their Kingdom Promises are fulfilled. This will happen at the return of their Messiah which will be at the end of the Tribulation. So, all believing Israel will be saved. In the meantime, God's mercy is offered to both Jew and Gentile alike in this Dispensation of Grace.

In the remainder of Romans, we see the practical application of everything we learned in the previous chapters. In chapter 12, Paul teaches the importance for believers to submit to God and the importance of loving fellow believers. That would be the social aspect; then there is the civil aspect. We are taught to be in submission to human government and love our neighbors as ourselves. In chapters 13 through 15, Paul discusses issues concerning our interaction with the weaker brother. We are to show the love of Christ by not judging or offending the weaker brother, showing charity, longsuffering, patience, kindness, and gentleness in teaching the weaker brother.

In chapters 15 and 16, we see Paul's benedictions. There are actually three benedictions in the last chapter. Paul shares his concern for believers. He wants them to be filled with the knowledge of the fullness of Christ and warns them to *mark* or identify corrupt teachers. They must avoid such teachers of doctrine contrary to Scripture. Finally, he desires to present them faultless before his Christ at His Appearing.

# 1

## Romans 1 (Part I)

We will go through the Book of Romans verse-by-verse starting at the beginning. Romans 1–2:

> **1 Paul, a servant of Jesus Christ, called to be an apostle, separated unto the gospel of God, 2 (Which he had promised afore by his prophets in the holy scriptures,)**

Paul begins with a statement of facts. He is a servant of Jesus Christ and he was called to be an apostle. What does it mean to be "called to be an apostle?" There are certain qualifications that have to be met in order to be "called to be an Apostle." The first qualification is he had to have met the resurrected Christ to be appointed by Him. Paul met the risen Christ on the Road to Damascus.

Let us look at Acts 9:1–6:

1 And Saul, yet breathing out threatenings and slaughter against the disciples of the Lord, went unto the high priest, 2 And desired of him letters to Damascus to the synagogues, that if he found any of this way, whether they were men or women, he might bring them bound unto Jerusalem.

3 And as he journeyed, he came near Damascus: and suddenly there shined round about him a light from heaven: 4 And he fell to the earth, and heard a voice saying unto him, Saul, Saul, why persecutest thou me?

5 And he said, Who art thou, Lord? And the Lord said, I am Jesus whom thou persecutest: it is hard for thee to kick against the pricks. 6 And he trembling and astonished said, Lord, what wilt thou have me to do? And the Lord said unto him, Arise, and go into the city, and it shall be told thee what thou must do.

What just happened here? Paul saw the glorified

Lord. Luke, who is recording the story for us, states there was a light that was brighter than the sun. Who was it that Paul saw? He saw the risen Lord. Now, that is one qualification for being an apostle, but let us look at another verse to demonstrate that Paul did actually see the Lord.

Look at 1 Corinthians. He speaks of Christ's death, burial, and resurrection. Then he lists all the people who saw him and he includes himself last of all. Notice his meeting was out of different circumstances. 1 Corinthians 15:7–8:

> **7 After that, he was seen of James; then of all the apostles. 8 And last of all he was seen of me also, as of one born out of due time.**

Paul writes in this epistle that he, in fact, did see the Lord!

There is one more qualification to verify the credentials for an apostle or prophet. They must be able to do signs and wonders. 2 Corinthians 12:11–12:

> **11 I am become a fool in glorying; ye have compelled me: for I ought to have been commended of you: for in nothing**

**am I behind the very chiefest apostles, though I be nothing.** 12 **Truly the signs of an apostle were wrought among you in all patience, in signs, and wonders, and mighty deeds.**

Another qualification to be an apostle was the ability to do signs and wonders. With the inspired Word now complete, no one today can meet the qualifications to be an apostle. Yet, the Apostle Paul did. The word *apostle* means *messenger* or *one sent as a messenger*. Therefore, Paul was legitimately called by the Lord Jesus Christ to be an apostle, but what was his message?

We could all say that God has sent us to be witnesses for the gospel. However, it was a unique commissioning for Paul. It is a special sending to be "called to be an apostle." This special sending came directly from the Lord Jesus Christ. To say anything less would diminish the importance of Paul's commissioning. Yet, in spite of this, Paul calls himself "a servant of Jesus Christ" when he discloses the purpose of his commission. He starts out by stating that he was called to be an apostle "separated unto the gospel of God." The word *gospel* means *good news*. However, there is more than one type of gospel or one type of good news in the word of God. Later, we will see that Paul was separated from the Twelve. He was called to be the Apostle to the Gentiles, also known as the Uncircumcision. Peter, James, John, and the others were called as Apostles to the Jews, also known as the Circumcision. This may be difficult for many to accept. We will see, without a shadow of a doubt, that Paul was to be the Apostle to the Gentiles with a message distinctly different from the other Twelve.

Paul received the Gospel of the Grace of God, the Gospel to the Gentiles. He states that clearly in the opening of his Letter to Romans saying he was *"separated unto the gospel of God."* The Gospel of God is the good news of Jesus Christ from the Old Testament. It is not the revelation of the mystery which Paul will explain later in this letter. That is why, in verse 2, he says, "which he had promised afore by his Prophets in the holy scriptures." The facts of Messiah's death, burial, and resurrection were well-known at that time. The Gospel of Grace to which Paul was separated by God was sent for the Gentiles. 1 Corinthians 15:3–4:

> 3 For I delivered unto you first of all that which I also received, how that Christ died for our sins according to the scriptures; 4 And that he was buried, and that he rose again the third day according to the scriptures:

From the first, Paul says he delivered the facts *according to the Scriptures*. What Scriptures would these be? They were the Scripture that existed at that time which we call the Old Testament. This same Jesus Who is the Messiah is also the Savior of the Gentiles. That is the reason he calls it *the Gospel of God*. The prophecies about Christ's death, burial, and resurrection were not fully understood by anyone. As previously stated, this is not "the revelation of the mystery" which Paul reveals later on. The "revelation of the mystery" is what Christ accomplished for the Gentiles by the Cross. This was *never* revealed in the Old Testament and *never* mentioned in prophecy. For this reason, Paul would later call it a *mystery*. God would first reveal it to the Apostle Paul. We cannot preach Christ, according to the "revelation of the mystery," without first understanding Who Jesus is from the prophecies of the Old Testament concerning His death, burial, and resurrection.

This is made clear for us in Scripture. Paul would go into the synagogues first and preach the Christ from the Old Testament. Shortly after his conversion on the road to Damascus. Acts 9:10–19:

> 10 **And there was a certain disciple at Damascus, named Ananias; and to him said the Lord in a vision, Ananias. And he said, Behold, I am here, Lord.** 11 **And**

the Lord said unto him, Arise, and go into the street which is called Straight, and enquire in the house of Judas for one called Saul, of Tarsus: for, behold, he prayeth, 12 And hath seen in a vision a man named Ananias coming in, and putting his hand on him, that he might re- ceive his sight. 13 Then Ananias answered, Lord, I have heard by many of this man, how much evil he hath done to thy saints at Jerusalem: 14 And here he hath authority from the chief priests to bind all that call on thy name.

15 But the Lord said unto him, Go thy way: for he is a chosen vessel unto me, to bear my name before the Gentiles, and kings, and the children of Israel: 16 For I will shew him how great things he must suffer for my name's sake.

17 And Ananias went his way, and entered into the house; and putting his hands on him said, Brother Saul, the Lord, even Jesus, that appeared unto thee in the way as thou camest, hath sent me, that thou mightest receive thy sight, and be filled with the Holy Ghost.

18 And immediately there fell from his eyes as it had been scales: and he received sight forthwith, and arose, and was baptized. 19 And when he had received meat, he was strengthened. Then was Saul certain days with the disciples which were at Damascus.

Notice where Paul goes immediately to begin his ministry. Verses 20–22:

20 And straightway he preached Christ in the synagogues, that he is the Son of God. 21 But all that heard him were amazed, and said; Is not this he that destroyed them which called on this name in Jerusalem, and came hither for that intent, that he might bring them bound unto the chief priests? 22 But Saul increased the more in strength, and confounded the Jews which dwelt at Damascus, proving that this is very Christ [Messiah].

Paul goes into the synagogues and immediately preaches Christ, that He is the son of God. This is the first phase of Paul's ministry. Acts 17: 1–4:

1 Now when they had passed through

**Amphipolis and Apollonia, they came to Thessalonica, where was a synagogue of the Jews: 2 And Paul, as his manner was, went in unto them, and three sabbath days reasoned with them out of the scriptures, 3 Opening and alleging, that Christ must needs have suffered, and risen again from the dead; and that this Jesus, whom I preach unto you, is Christ. 4 And some of them believed, and consorted with Paul and Silas; and of the devout Greeks a great multitude, and of the chief women not a few.**

This is another reference of Paul going into the synagogue and preaching that Jesus is the Messiah. He goes into detail from the Old Testament Law, Prophets, and Writings that Jesus is the Son of God; that He was crucified, was buried, and He rose again the third day.

After Paul preaches his initial message to the Jews, what is his next step? For the answer, we need to look at Acts 13: 26–27:

**26 Men and brethren, children of the stock of Abraham, and whosoever among you feareth God, to you is the**

word of this salvation sent. 27 For they that dwell at Jerusalem, and their rulers, because they knew him not, nor yet the voices of the prophets which are read every sabbath day, they have fulfilled them in condemning him.

The Jews did not understand what the Old Testament Law and Prophet said concerning their Messiah's birth, death, and resurrection. Verses 28–33:

28 And though they found no cause of [reason for] death in him, yet desired they Pilate that he should be slain. 29 And when they had fulfilled all that was written of him, they took him down from the tree, and laid him in a sepulchre.

30 But God raised him from the dead: 31 And he was seen many days of them which came up with him from Galilee to Jerusalem, who are his witnesses unto the people. 32 And we declare unto you glad tidings, how that the promise which was made unto the fathers, 33 God hath fulfilled the same unto us their children, in that he hath raised up Jesus again; as it is also written in the

**second psalm, Thou art my Son, this day have I begotten thee.**

The word "begotten" refers to a birth from a "resurrection from the dead." In Revelation, we are told Jesus Christ, Who is the faithful witness, is the first begotten from the dead. (See Revelation 1:5.)

Let us continue. Verses 34–37:

**34 And as concerning that he raised him up from the dead, now no more to return to corruption, he said on this wise, I will give you the sure mercies of David. 35 Wherefore he saith also in another psalm, Thou shalt not suffer thine Holy One to see corruption. 36 For David, after he had served his own generation by the will of God, fell on sleep, and was laid unto his fathers, and saw corruption: 37 But he, whom God raised again, saw no corruption.**

Later, Paul quotes David to make it clear that God will one day give Israel the sure mercies of David and remember Israel's sins no more. That is prophetic and not part of the mystery. Note to whom Paul is speaking in the following verses as he refers to them as *men and brethren*. They are the Jews which

Paul is addressing. Continue with verses 38–43:

> 38 Be it known unto you therefore, men and brethren, that through this man is preached unto you the forgiveness of sins: 39 And by him all that believe are justified from all things, from which ye could not be justified by the law of Moses. 40 Beware therefore, lest that come upon you, which is spoken of in the prophets; 41 Behold, ye despisers, and wonder, and perish: for I work a work in your days, a work which ye shall in no wise believe, though a man declare it unto you.
>
> 42 And when the Jews were gone out of the synagogue, the Gentiles besought that these words might be preached to them the next sabbath. 43 Now when the congregation was broken up, many of the Jews and religious proselytes followed Paul and Barnabas: who, speaking to them, persuaded them to continue in the grace of God.

Paul first explained Who Jesus is from the Old Testament. It was prophesied that He would be crucified, buried, and rise again from the grave. Then, he begins to explain to these Jews that they could now be justified by grace without the Law. He begins to teach them about "the revelation of the mystery."

Here is something we need to understand when we look at Romans 1. Some people will tell you that Paul was preaching the Gospel of the Kingdom all the way to Acts 28. However, that is not the case. Paul is, first, teaching the Jews to understand Who Jesus is from the Old Testament. There was a reason He must be crucified according to the will of God fulfilling all prophecy. They needed a foundation upon which to build their understanding. That foundation is Jesus Christ and the Cross. Upon that foundation, Paul would build by preaching Jesus Christ according to "the revelation of the mystery."

Now, let us go back to Romans 1. Paul builds upon the Jews' foundational understanding by presenting the revelation of the mystery which he received. Romans 1:5–6:

> 4 **And declared to be the Son of God with power, according to the spirit of holiness, by the resurrection from the dead:** 5 **By whom we have received grace and apostleship, for obedience to the faith among all nations, for his name:** 6 **Among whom are ye also the called of**

**Jesus Christ:**

Notice that he says, "we have received grace." Further, it is now available to *all nations* which means *all people* – both Jews and non-Jews. How is this possible? It is available to all through *obedience to the faith* which means *believing*. We can all received God's grace by *believing* the Gospel of Grace. Normally, when we think of *obedience*, we think about complying with a task that must be performed. However, in this case, it is not a task that we must perform, but rather the doctrine we must believe. Christ "humbled himself, and became obedient unto death, even the death of the cross" (Phil. 2:8). Now, *obedience to the faith* is accomplished by *believing*.

We need to believe the Gospel of Grace: that Christ died for our sins, was buried, and rose again for our justification on the third day. Paul writes "among whom are ye also the *called* of Jesus Christ." We are *called* to be saints. Verse 7:

> 7 **To all that be in Rome, beloved of God, called to be saints: Grace to you and peace from God our Father, and the Lord Jesus Christ.**

Everybody that believes the gospel is a saint. Sainthood is not something that is acquired through good deeds or by being a good person. Sainthood is something to which we are called when we believe the gospel. The word *sainthood* is from the term *sanctification*. Being *sanctified* is about *being separated*, being *called-out* for God's purposes. That is what it means to be a saint. It is to the saints in Rome that Paul is writing this epistle. He ends his greeting by blessing them with grace and peace from God our Father and the Lord Jesus Christ. However, this is not just some greeting or salutation that was part of the culture. This goes far beyond a cultural greeting.

Paul is teaching something. In the beginning of each of his epistles, he includes the words: *grace* and *peace*. He wants to emphasize the point that we are now in the dispensation in which both the *grace of God* and the *peace with God* abound. This is exactly the opposite of judgment and wrath. Paul declares this in each of his letters. We are living in the dispensation of God's glorious grace and peace. We are not under wrath and judgment today. We are under grace and peace! His teaching or doctrine makes this very clear.

We continue. Verse 8:

**8 First, I thank my God through Jesus Christ for you all, that your faith is spoken of throughout the whole world.**

It says, "your faith is spoken of throughout the whole world." Their faith is in the Gospel of Grace. It is being spoken about or known throughout "the whole world." Here is an important dispensational point. The Twelve came to Jesus and asked Him a question. Matthew 24:3:

> 3 **And as he sat upon the mount of Olives, the disciples came unto him privately, saying, Tell us, when shall these things be? and what shall be the sign of thy coming, and of the end of the world?**

Notice the question concerns the end of the world and the Second Coming of Christ. Therefore, it has to do with the time during the Tribulation at the end of the world. Here is Jesus' response. Matthew 24:14:

> 14 **And this gospel of the kingdom shall be preached in all the world for a witness unto all nations; and then shall the end come.**

Christ says the Gospel of the Kingdom will be preached in all the world; then the end will come. There is a problem when someone tries to make the Gospel of Grace the same gospel as the Gospel of the Kingdom. They are combining two totally separate dispensations!

Paul writes in Romans 1:8 that the gospel that he is preaching, by which they are saved, is spoken of *throughout the whole world.* If Paul is talking about the Gospel of the Kingdom in Romans 1, then why did the end not come? Let us look at a couple more verses on this. Colossians 1:1–2:

> 1 **Paul, an apostle of Jesus Christ by the will of God, and Timotheus our brother, 2 To the saints and faithful brethren in Christ which are at Colosse: Grace be unto you, and peace, from God our Father and the Lord Jesus Christ.**

Notice this salutation also includes the words "Grace be unto you and peace, from God our Father and the Lord Jesus Christ." Verses 3–6:

> 3 **We give thanks to God and the Father of our Lord Jesus Christ, praying always for you, 4 Since we heard of your faith in Christ Jesus, and of the love which ye have to all the saints, 5 For the hope which is laid up for you in heaven, whereof ye heard before in the word of the truth of the gospel; 6 <u>Which is come unto you, as it is in all the world;</u> and**

**bringeth forth fruit, as it doth also in you, since the day ye heard of it, and knew the grace of God in truth:**

Speaking of the truth of the Gospel of Grace, it has come to the Colossians "as it is in all the world." So, Paul's gospel was made known throughout the whole ancient world during his lifetime. Therefore, it cannot be the Gospel of the Kingdom.

Let us return to Romans 1:9–11:

**9 For God is my witness, whom I serve with my spirit in the gospel of his Son, that without ceasing I make mention of you always in my prayers; 10 Making request, if by any means now at length I might have a prosperous journey by the will of God to come unto you. 11 For I long to see you, that I may impart unto you some spiritual gift, to the end ye may be established;**

Paul states here and in other letters that he prayed *without ceasing*. What does it mean to pray without ceasing? People have different ideas. Some people think it has to do with prayerful thoughts; not actually speaking to the Lord verbally. I think what Paul is really communicating here is the idea that we should never stop praying. He writes *making request*, because when he has something on his mind, he is continually in prayer about it. He wants a prosperous journey with the result of coming to Rome. Unfortunately, some charismatic preachers will misuse this verse to say that Paul's prayer for "a prosperous journey" is about his desire to get rich. It is not about money. Here the word *prosperous* is used in a spiritual sense meaning spiritual *success*. Paul wants a successful journey according to the will of God.

Paul longs to see believers established in the faith so that they may use that faith to encourage each other. Verse 12:

> 12 **That is, that I may be comforted to-gether with you by the mutual faith both of you and me.**

In comforting each other, Paul too will be comforted. In the Gospel of John, the Lord says that the Holy Spirit is the Comforter. What does the Holy Spirit use to bring comfort? He uses the Scriptures. It is His number one source of comfort. Romans 15:4:

> 4 **For whatsoever things were written aforetime were written for our learning, that we through patience and comfort of the scriptures might have hope.**

The ministry of the Holy Spirit is to bring comfort and the way He brings comfort is through the Word of God. Our comfort is through the hope we receive from the Scriptures. Paul wants to be comforted from the Scriptures together with the believers in Rome by their mutual faith in the Gospel of Grace. Another way the Holy Spirit brings comfort is through the fellowship of other like-minded believers. The encouragement, admonishment, and sharing that one receives from other believers is another way the Holy Spirit works today. Romans 1:13:

**13 Now I would not have you ignorant, brethren, that oftentimes I purposed to come unto you, (but was let hitherto,) that I might have some fruit among you also, even as among other Gentiles.**

Paul does not want the believers in Rome to be unaware of his attempts to come to them for a visit. He says he was *let hitherto*. The verb *to let* is an old English word meaning "the power or authority to allow or prevent." The word hitherto which means "up until this point in time." So, Paul, up until this point has been prevented or hindered to coming to them each time he proposed to do so. He desired to have some fruit among them as he had with other Gentiles.

Paul started his ministry by focusing on the

Jews first, but that will change. Verse 14:

**14 I am debtor both to the Greeks, and to the Barbarians; both to the wise, and to the unwise.**

Paul wants the believers in Rome to understand that he needed to deal with the Jews first. A group of unbelieving Jews are always trying to hinder Paul's ministry. His ministry is to the Jew first because God instructed him to go to them first. However, God gave Paul the task of being the Apostle to the Gentiles. With that in mind, Paul writes "I am debtor both to the Greeks and to the Barbarians." Then, he continues "both to the wise and to the unwise." Paul is using two sets of words for the purpose of a comparison. The Greeks were known for their human wisdom and the barbarians were considered uneducated. So *the wise* would be the Greeks because the Greeks worshiped human wisdom and philosophy, although they were not spiritually wise. The Greek culture idolized education and human wisdom. The Barbarians were just the opposite. They were unlearned and uncivilized. To both of these distinct groups of Gentiles, Paul says he is their *debtor* concerning the Gospel of Grace.

We continue. Verse 15:

**15 So, as much as in me is, I am ready to preach the gospel to you that are at Rome also.**

Paul commits to coming to see them in Rome and, thereby, not leaving them out of his personal instruction. His missionary journeys are the basis for his preaching the Gospel of Grace. He plans to go to Rome, but he must first go by way of Jerusalem. He made a pledge to support the destitute saints in Jerusalem who followed the Kingdom Gospel.

We will continue with the rest of Romans 1 in the next chapter.

# 2

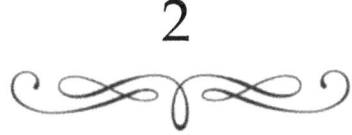

## Romans 1 (Part II)

We left Paul planning his journey to Rome after he brings the financial gift to the Kingdom Believers in Jerusalem. Remember Paul's care for his fellow Jews as he would always preach to them first. Let us continue. Romans 1:16:

> 16 **For I am not ashamed of the gospel of Christ: for it is the power of God unto salvation to every one that believeth; to the Jew first, and also to the Greek.**

Paul is not ashamed of the Gospel of Grace. He will bring his gospel to anyone whether they are Jews or Gentiles, called *Greeks* above. Paul is a Jew himself and it was considered scandalous for any Jew to associate with Gentiles. It is true that he was neither ashamed nor afraid to proclaim the good news of the Gospel of Grace to anyone. The truth of this gospel is the power unto salvation to both the Jew and the Gentile alike.

Paul knew full well from experience that he would be going against the current Jewish establishment. He would be their enemy, but he was not concerned what anyone would think of him. Verse 17:

**17 For therein is the righteousness of God revealed from faith to faith: as it is written, The just shall live by faith.**

The Gospel of Grace is the righteousness of God. How is it revealed? It says *from faith to faith*. In Genesis, God declared Abraham righteous by faith. Noah was also justified by faith and God declared him righteous. He declared David righteous, not by works, but by faith. As we consider Israel's history, we find different people who were declared righteous by God because of their faith. Here is a question: Did they know the Gospel of Jesus Christ?

None of the prophecies about the death, burial, and resurrection of Christ were understood. Let me make this clear. We are not talking about the "revelation of the mystery, which God kept secret since the world began" and was revealed to the Apostle Paul. There is no evidence in either the Old Testament or the four Gospels about the preaching of Jesus Christ according to the "revelation of the mystery." However, there are prophecies in the Old Testament which are explained in the Gospels about Christ's death, burial, and resurrection. Did Adam and Eve understand the Cross? Did Noah understand the Cross? Did Abraham understand the Cross? No. Neither did David understand the Cross. Even the Twelve did not understand Jesus when He told them He was going to suffer and die. People throughout the Old Testament had faith in what God had revealed to them at that time. Although they did not fully understand, God honored their faith and saved them. Why did they not understand? It is because the Cross has nothing to do with the Gospel of the Kingdom.

God knew Christ would go to the Cross and die for the sins of the world. He could justify them on the basis of the Cross when they put their faith in what God had revealed to them at that time. This is what Paul means when he writes "therein is the righteousness of God," the Gospel of Christ which is "revealed from faith to faith." Then, Paul refers to a Scripture written to the Jews by the prophet Habakkuk, "but the just shall live by his faith" (Hab. 2:4). Later, in the Book of Hebrews which is written to believing Jews, it repeats this. "Now the just shall live by faith" (Heb. 10:38).

Therefore, everyone who had faith in God's promises had God impute His righteousness to them based on the future work of the Cross. They were not saved by grace through faith in the Cross for they did not know anything about it. Some people claim that everyone in every age is saved by grace alone. That is not true. Believing Jews must express their faith by following the Law and doing good works as proof of their active faith. Their works will not save them. What will save them is their active faith!

Let us continue. Verse 18:

**18 For the wrath of God is revealed from heaven against all ungodliness and unrighteousness of men, who hold the truth in unrighteousness;**

The Gospel of Grace allows God to impute the righteousness of His Son to us. Today, we put our faith in what Christ did for us on the Cross. God is a righteous God and sin must be judged. Therefore, the penalty for our sin must be paid. On the Cross, the Lord Jesus Christ took our sin and our punishment upon Himself. At the Cross, we can see the wrath of God being poured out upon His Son. God reveals His righteousness by having Jesus go to the Cross. At the same time, we see the obedience of His Son Who fulfilled the requirements of the Father to permanently deal with Sin.

Look at John 18:11–14:

> **11 Then said Jesus unto Peter, Put up thy sword into the sheath: <u>the cup which my Father hath given me, shall I not drink it?</u> 12 Then the band and the captain and officers of the Jews took Jesus, and bound him, 13 And led him away to Annas first; for he was father in law to Caiaphas, which was the high priest that same year. 14 Now Caiaphas was he, which gave counsel to the Jews, that <u>it was expedient that one man should die for the people.</u>**

The cup given to Jesus on the Cross was the cup of "the wrath of God." (See Revelation 14:8–10.) As Christ suffered on the Cross, "the wrath of God" was poured out upon His righteous Son.

Now, God was able to impute the righteousness of His Son to others based upon faith. They will never need to experience "the wrath of God" because they believe. Romans 5:8-9:

> **8 But God commendeth his love toward us, in that, while we were yet sinners,**

**Christ died for us. 9 Much more then, being now justified by his blood, we shall be saved from wrath through him.**

Remember this: Jesus Christ took God's wrath upon Himself at the Cross. Romans 1:18–19:

> **18 For the wrath of God is revealed from heaven against all ungodliness and unrighteousness of men, who hold the truth in unrighteousness; 19 Because that which may be known of God is manifest in them; for God hath shewed it unto them.**

The "wrath of God" was revealed at the Cross. One might ask, "What about God's wrath on Sodom and Gomorrah? Wasn't that God's wrath? How about the flood?" Yes, that was God's wrath and judgment resulted. However, it was upon the Cross where "the wrath of God" was satisfied based upon the faithfulness of Christ. It was the Cross that demonstrated to the world and also the heavenly realms that the payment for sin was made. No one knew this at the time until Christ revealed this mystery to Paul. He writes about this in his letters.

There are those who do not want to acknowledge the truth of God's righteousness. They do not want to accept the truth and choose to reject it. They use the word *science* which means *knowledge*. It specifically refers to man's knowledge. Paul says that this *science* is falsely called so. They make up things and try to cover up the truth. In Romans 1, we read about those "who hold the truth in unrighteousness." This means "in unbelief." They are willfully disobedient to a gracious God. Why? It is because of all the evidence which God makes available to them daily. The fulness of His Creation is self-evident. They can see His Creation, but they choose to ignore it.

How can someone who has never read a Bible, never heard a sermon preached, never attended a church service, know God? All creatures should inherently know their Creator. They should know there is a God, but they choose to ignore or reject Him. What else could they also know? Romans 2:13–16:

> 13 **(For not the hearers of the law are just before God, but the doers of the law shall be justified. 14 For when the Gentiles, which have not the law, do by nature the things contained in the law, these, having not the law, are a law unto themselves: 15 Which shew the work of the law written in their hearts, their**

**conscience also bearing witness, and their thoughts the mean while accusing or else excusing one another;) 16 In the day when God shall judge the secrets of men by Jesus Christ according to my gospel.**

Remember, the Gentiles were never given the Law of Moses. However, everyone has "the work of the law written in their hearts." How is this possible? It is because God gave all men a conscience: the ability to know the difference between right and wrong. Everyone knows there is a God. They know it naturally; they know it inherently. No one can look at Creation and say there is no God. They know the difference between right from wrong and they also know there are consequences for their actions. Wrong must be punished. This is evident in their own accusations. For that reason, Paul says, "their conscience also bearing witness and their thoughts the mean while accusing or else excusing one another." So, people naturally judge each other, either accusing or excusing each other. If a person does something wrong in this life, then who is to administer justice? In other words, who is to punish the wrong-doer? God instituted human government for that purpose.

Paul will later talk about the powers that are

ordained by God. Romans 13:5-7:

> 5 **Wherefore ye must needs be subject, not only for wrath, but also for conscience sake. 6 For this cause pay ye tribute also: for they are God's ministers, attending continually upon this very thing. 7 Render therefore to all their dues: tribute to whom tribute is due; custom to whom custom; fear to whom fear; honour to whom honour.**

Since our strong feeling that wrong must be punished, Paul writes "not only for wrath." Here, the word *wrath* means *punishment*. He points out the principal reason for this by reminding us it is "for conscience sake." It is our inherent conscience which God gave to us all that tells us there is right and wrong.

Let us return to Romans 1. In the following verses, Paul builds a case against mankind. It is based upon their responses to God's goodness and graciousness. Romans 1:19–20:

> 19 **Because that which may be known of God is manifest in them; for God hath shewed it unto them. 20 For the invisible things of him from the creation of the**

**world are clearly seen, being understood by the things that are made, even his eternal power and Godhead; so that they are without excuse:**

These things are inherently known about God because they can see "the invisible things of him" since "the creation of the world." Since the beginning they have been seen and *understood.* Therefore, Man is without excuse. He has no defense. He cannot say, "I didn't know." With God, there will be no excuse!

We continue. Verse 21:

**21 Because that, when they knew God, they glorified him not as God, neither were thankful; but became vain in their imaginations, and their foolish heart was darkened.**

Although mankind undeniably knew God, they chose neither to acknowledge God nor glorify Him. It was a choice then and it is a choice people make today. They would neither glorify Him nor thank Him. This is a central point with Paul. Being thankful to God is important. Paul talks about thankfulness to God more than any other doctrine in his letters. Why is that? By being thankful, we both acknowledge God for Who He is and what He has done for us.

When we stop being thankful to God, we get in trouble. Then, by sin nature, we will go back to corrupt thoughts. That is just our default. Throughout the Bible, we see this pattern. Paul tells us the result of their rejection. Their *foolish heart* became darkened. Again, if we are not being thankful, if we are not acknowledging God, then we will become vain in our imaginations and our foolish hearts will be darkened.

What is the result of hearts that become darkened? The word *vain* used above is defined as *having or showing an excessively high opinion of one's appearance, abilities, or worth*. How does becoming *vain* affect them? Verse 22:

22 **Professing themselves to be wise, they became fools,**

People who think they are wise invent ways to remove the Creator from Creation. They use the Big Bang Theory to teach the effect, but they fail to explain the cause. Others follow Darwin's theory that the origin of man was from monkeys. If we ask them the origin of monkeys, then they lose their patience and get angry. It is their way of getting rid of God. It is necessary for them to avoid what is obvious. There is a Creator and we, as creatures, are subject to Him.

Then, they fashion a false substitute for God

which is of their own creation. Verse 23:

> 23 **And changed the glory of the uncor-**
> **ruptible God into an image made like to**
> **corruptible man, and to birds, and four-**
> **footed beasts, and creeping things.**

I believe that demons or fallen angels played a part
in substituting the glory of the *uncorruptible God* into
images or idols. These idols are actually substitute
gods whereby these fallen angels or demons receive
worship to themselves. Men worship what they create; not the Creator. This applies today too. Verses
24–25:

> 24 **Wherefore God also gave them up to**
> **uncleanness through the lusts of their**
> **own hearts, to dishonour their own**
> **bodies between themselves: 25 Who**
> **changed the truth of God into a lie, and**
> **worshipped and served the creature**
> **more than the Creator, who is blessed**
> **for ever. Amen.**

In his vanity, man got into the issue of sexual
perversion. They exchanged truth for a lie. In doing
so they took that which is due to the Creator and, instead, gave their worship and service to what they
themselves had created. This passage has a story be-

hind it, an historical application which goes back to Genesis 6. Yet, it also has an individual application. Each of us can go down this same horrible road. We must never stop thanking God for Who He is. Verses 26–27:

> 26 For this cause God gave them up unto vile affections: for even their women did change the natural use into that which is against nature: 27 And likewise also the men, leaving the natural use of the woman, burned in their lust one toward another; men with men working that which is unseemly, and receiving in themselves that recompence of their error which was meet [appropriate].

Paul is talking about gross sexual perversions of all sorts. Paul is saying that they will receive *recompense* which means *compensation* or *repayment* for their sinful actions. Every man is endowed by God with a conscience. This is God's moral law that demands consequences. In this case, that would be punishment. The word *meet* above means *appropriate* thereby letting the punishment fit the crime.

God's righteousness requires that He dispense the right or proper punishment when needed. Verse 28:

**28 And even as they did not like to retain God in their knowledge, God gave them over to a reprobate mind, to do those things which are not convenient;**

The word *convenient* is not used in its current meaning of fitting in well with one's personal needs, activities, and plans. Rather, it means *fitting, proper, or appropriate*. In other words, it refers to actions which are acceptable to God and meet His intent of acceptable behavior for His Creatures.

The issue is not whether they can understand or that they need proof of God's existence. Using their free will, they have willingly chosen not to retain God it in their knowledge. If someone has chosen not to retain God in their knowledge, God will not give them *more light* than they already have. Some people ask, "Well, what about a tribe in some remote corner of the world who has never heard the name of Jesus?" Here is the answer: God instilled the conscience in every man since the expulsion of man from the Garden of Eden. The knowledge of God and the knowledge of right and wrong are part of the inner man. They are to listen to it regardless of whether they have the saving knowledge of Jesus Christ. God is just. He will judge them according to their knowledge of God. Paul will deal with this in greater detail later on.

Earlier, when I mentioned the Big Bang Theory, I stated that the theorists express the effect without ever explaining the cause. That was true. However, that is not the case with Paul's indictment of mankind. He has included an explanation, in great detail, of the cause of man's state. That is man's determination to ignore God and remove their Creator in their knowledge. Now, he lists the effect of their choice. Verses 29–31:

> 29 **Being filled with all unrighteousness, fornication, wickedness, covetousness, maliciousness; full of envy, murder, debate, deceit, malignity; whisperers,** 30 **Backbiters, haters of God, despiteful, proud, boasters, inventors of evil things, disobedient to parents,** 31 **Without understanding, covenant-breakers, without natural affection, implacable, unmerciful:**

If someone chooses not to retain or reject God in their knowledge, then right or wrong does not matter. So, they end up as rebellious and ungrateful children. How many babies have been aborted by choice in the world? Think of late-term abortions or even after-birth abortions? This is a case of parents being without natural affection. The word *implacable* means *unable to be appeased.* They are angry and hostile. They are *unmerciful* which means *cruel, harsh,* and *showing no mercy*. Without God, nothing can appease them so they heap more misery upon themselves and others.

Paul concludes with this. Although they know that, according to their conscience, there are consequences for their actions, they not only do wrong, but delight in others who do wrong as well. Verse 32:

> 32 **Who knowing the judgment of God, that they which commit such things are worthy of death, not only do the same, but have pleasure in them that do them.**

# 3

## Romans 2

Before we start, I would like us to look at something again. Paul revealed the condition of man. He provided a list showing his downward spiral into sin. There is a reason I am repeating this. This is God's indictment of mankind. Romans 1:28–32:

> 28 **And even as they did not like to retain God in their knowledge, God gave them over to a reprobate mind, to do those things which are not convenient;** 29 **Being filled with all unrighteousness, fornication, wickedness, covetousness, maliciousness; full of envy, murder, debate, deceit, malignity; whisperers,** 30 **Backbiters, haters of God, despiteful, proud, boasters, inventors of evil things, disobedient to parents,** 31 **Without understanding, covenant-breakers,**

without natural affection, implacable, unmerciful: 32 Who knowing the judgment of God, that they which commit such things are worthy of death, not only do the same, but have pleasure in them that do them.

Paul begins Romans 2 with the word *therefore*. With everything he just wrote in the preceding chapter, he comes to a conclusion. Romans 2:1:

1 Therefore thou art inexcusable, O man, whosoever thou art that judgest: for wherein thou judgest another, thou condemnest thyself; for thou that judgest doest the same things.

We cannot condemn someone else for doing the same thing we do ourselves. In doing so, we also condemn ourselves. Everybody has sinned against God and, therefore, everybody is guilty. Verses 2–3:

2 But we are sure that the judgment of God is according to truth against them which commit such things. 3 And thinkest thou this, O man, that judgest them which do such things, and doest the same, that thou shalt escape the judgment of God?

Paul makes an important point. People judge others even though they do the same thing themselves. Yet, while being in need of salvation, they reject God's goodness. Verse 4:

> 4 **Or despisest thou the riches of his goodness and forbearance and longsuffering; not knowing that the goodness of God leadeth thee to repentance?**

He speaks about God's goodness, forbearance, and long-suffering in spite of man's sin and rebellion. It is the goodness of God that causes us to have a change of mind and a renewal of heart. Verse 5:

> 5 **But after thy hardness and impenitent heart treasurest up unto thyself wrath against the day of wrath and revelation of the righteous judgment of God;**

Everybody is in the same boat when it comes to sin. There is no one who is righteous; no not one. Everybody is guilty. So the right attitude is to be humble. We are all sinners and need God's mercy. We need His grace.

Let us go to the Gospel of Luke where the Lord is telling a parable. Luke 18:10–13:

10 Two men went up into the temple to pray; the one a Pharisee, and the other a publican. 11 The Pharisee stood and prayed thus with himself, God, I thank thee, that I am not as other men are, extortioners, unjust, adulterers, or even as this publican. 12 I fast twice in the week, I give tithes of all that I possess. 13 And the publican, standing afar off, would not lift up so much as his eyes unto heaven, but smote upon his breast, saying, God be merciful to me a sinner.

This Pharisee is like the person that Paul described above. He judges others because he thinks he is better. Yet he condemns himself when he judges the other. Verse 14:

14 I tell you, this man went down to his house justified rather than the other: for every one that exalteth himself shall be abased; and he that humbleth himself shall be exalted.

Here is the point. The publican had the right attitude. He saw himself as a sinner and in need of God's mercy. We should have the same attitude also. We should never think that we have "somehow arrived," as they say, or think that we are somehow better than somebody else. We are not. Everybody is in the same boat. We all need God's mercy. We all need Christ and His salvation through the Cross.

There is only one way to be saved and that is to be in a right position with God. We cannot add to what Christ has already done. We must trust solely in what He has already completed for us on the Cross. What is "the goodness of God" to us? (Rom. 2:4). We will find the answer in Romans 11:22:

> **22 Behold therefore the goodness and severity of God: on them which fell, severity; but toward thee, goodness, if thou continue in his goodness: otherwise thou also shalt be cut off.**

Paul refers to Israel because they fell. The goodness of God for us, today, is having access to His offer of grace. This offer is available to everyone. He offers salvation through faith in what His Son did on the Cross. *That* is "the goodness of God."

God's goodness leads to a change of mind and a change of heart. We get to that point in our lives through the hearing of the Word of God. We realize that we do not deserve rewards for our actions. Instead; we deserve punishment. We learn that we receive salvation by trusting in what Christ did for us on the Cross. We recognized the state or condition we were in. We accepted His gift of salvation and now we are saved. We had gone our whole life thinking that we were fine and we do not need God. Then, we hear the Gospel of Grace. We learn that Christ died for our sins, was buried, and rose again the third day. And, we believe! That is how God's goodness leads to repentance. Romans 2:5:

> 5 But after thy hardness and impenitent heart treasurest up unto thyself wrath against the day of wrath and revelation of the righteous judgment of God;

The phrase "hardness and impenitent heart" means a heart that is fixed and unchanging. It is unwilling to show sorrow and remorse. In other words, it is a refusal to change or repent. It is a resolve to continue rejecting God and what God says. How do we define a *hard heart?* I want you to see from Scripture what it means. Look at Hebrews 3:15:

> 15 While it is said, To day if ye will hear his voice, harden not your hearts, as in the provocation.

This verse refers to the time when Israel was in the Wilderness during the Exodus from Egypt. It was critical for them to hear God's voice as He guided them through the Wilderness. Yet, they did not listen. By doing so, they provoked God to anger. Like children, they would not listen to their Father. How does this apply today? The verse above says, "Today, if ye will hear His voice, harden not your hearts." What is meant by *His voice?*

Look at John 10:27:

**27 My sheep hear my voice, and I know them, and they follow me:**

What does He mean by *His voice?* Is He talking about his literal audible voice? Well, yes, that is part of it, but it goes beyond that. Look at John 5:36–37:

**36 But I have greater witness than that of John: for the works which the Father hath given me to finish, the same works that I do, bear witness of me, that the Father hath sent me. 37 And the Father himself, which hath sent me, hath borne witness of me. Ye have neither heard his voice at any time, nor seen his shape.**

We will see how the Lord defines hearing His voice. John continues. Verses 38–39:

**38** And ye have not his word abiding in you: for whom he hath sent, him ye believe not. **39** Search the scriptures; for in them ye think ye have eternal life: and they are they which testify of me.

John summarizes. Verses 46–47:

**46** For had ye believed Moses, ye would have believed me: for he wrote of me. **47** But if ye believe not his writings, how shall ye believe my words?

Here is an important point. To hear the voice of God we must read and understand the Scriptures. These are the words God spoke that were written down in our Bible. If we are going to hear the voice of God, we have to read and understand God's Word. Therefore, when we think about reading the Bible, we are not to harden our hearts. To not hear the Scriptures is to reject the voice of God.

Let us continue. Romans 2:6–11:

**6** Who will render to every man according to his deeds: **7** To them who by patient continuance in well doing seek for glory and honour and immortality, eternal life: **8** But unto them that are contentious, and do not obey the truth, but obey unrighteousness, indignation and wrath, 9 Tribulation and anguish, upon every soul of man that doeth evil, of the Jew first, and also of the Gentile; 10 But glory, honour, and peace, to every man that worketh good, to the Jew first, and also to the Gentile: 11 For there is no respect of persons with God.

God is broadly applying His justice to all people without distinction. Verses 12–16:

12 For as many as have sinned without law shall also perish without law: and as many as have sinned in the law shall be judged by the law; 13 (For not the hearers of the law are just before God, but the doers of the law shall be justified. 14 For when the Gentiles, which have not the law, do by nature the things contained in the law, these, having not the law, are a law unto themselves: 15 Which shew the work of the law written in their hearts, their conscience also bearing witness, and their thoughts the mean while accusing or else excusing one another;) 16 In the day when God shall judge the secrets of

**men by Jesus Christ according to my gospel.**

When Paul chooses to use the phrase "according to my gospel," he refers to the Gospel of the Grace that was given to him by God.

Some people get confused about these verses. Let me suggest that they were written within an historical context. When Paul says that Jesus is the Judge over us all and He will "render to every man according to his deeds," he is talking about those people who did not know who Jesus was. Some traditional church-es teach that those in the Old Testament were looking forward to the Cross while those in the New Testament look back at the Cross. Well, that is not true. No one before the Cross knew anything about the Cross or Who Jesus was.

Look at Acts 17:22–31:

**22 Then Paul stood in the midst of Mars' hill, and said, Ye men of Athens, I perceive that in all things ye are too superstitious. 23 For as I passed by, and beheld your devotions, I found an altar with this inscription, TO THE UNKNOWN GOD. Whom therefore ye ignorantly worship, him declare I unto**

you. 24 God that made the world and all things therein, seeing that he is Lord of heaven and earth, dwelleth not in temples made with hands; 25 Neither is worshipped with men's hands, as though he needed any thing, seeing he giveth to all life, and breath, and all things; 26 And hath made of one blood all nations of men for to dwell on all the face of the earth, and hath determined the times before appointed, and the bounds of their habitation;

27 That they should seek the Lord, if haply they might feel after him, and find him, though he be not far from every one of us 28 For in him we live, and move, and have our being; as certain also of your own poets have said, For we are also his offspring. 29 Forasmuch then as we are the offspring of God, we ought not to think that the Godhead is like unto gold, or silver, or stone, graven by art and man's device.

30 And the times of this ignorance God winked at; but now commandeth all men every where to repent: 31 Because he hath appointed a day, in the which

**he will judge the world in righteous-
ness by that man whom he hath ordained; whereof he hath given assurance unto all men, in that he hath raised
him from the dead.**

In verse 30, Paul writes "and the times of this
ignorance God winked at." If we return to Romans 2,
I will make my point. When we read verses 6
through 12, this refers to a time when neither Jew nor
Gentile had any knowledge of Christ and the Cross.
He would be "seeking glory and honor and immortality eternal life," but he did it without the
knowledge of Christ and the Cross. In verse 10, he
writes "but glory, honor, and peace, to every man
that worketh good, to the Jew first, and also to the
Gentile." This refers to people seeking the truth,
seeking God, and seeking *more light.*

However, once the Apostle Paul revealed to
the whole world Christ and the Cross, then everybody is measured by that message. Everybody in the
world is then held accountable to what Paul has revealed. Prior to that, though people were seeking
more truth, God honored their faith in the light of the
truth they had been given. There was a time when
they could not know about the Cross. God winked at
their ignorance and honored their faith in what truth
He had revealed to them. Everybody was considered

ignorant by God's standard until Paul's revelation. Then, they learned about Christ and the Cross. (See Acts 17.) One might ask, "What about today? What about someone who has not heard about Christ and the Cross? What if they did not have access to that information?" God would judge them accordingly. This is because God is a righteous judge. He would judge them based upon what they could know at that time. At the minimum, they would be judged by how they lived according to their conscience.

As we receive more knowledge of the truth concerning Christ and the Cross, we are then held accountable to that next level of truth or revelation. Look back at Romans 2:13–15:

> 13 **(For not the hearers of the law are just before God, but the doers of the law shall be justified. 14 For when the Gentiles, which have not the law, do by nature the things contained in the law, these, having not the law, are a law unto themselves: 15 Which shew the work of the law written in their hearts, their conscience also bearing witness, and their thoughts the mean while accusing or else excusing one another;)**

That is what people do before they believe the gospel. Everybody does it. They may have never been given the Law of Moses, but everyone receives a conscience. They do what verse 15 explains above. It says that they sometimes accuse and sometimes excuse one another. We have this knowledge of right and wrong within us. The conscience is the basis upon which the Gentiles would be held accountable.

Let us move on. Verse 16:

**16 In the day when God shall judge the secrets of men by Jesus Christ according to my gospel.**

Notice what Paul calls the message of the Gospel of Grace which was given to him. He calls it *my gospel.* Is that not a curious thing considering there were twelve other apostles?

At this point Paul changes his attention from everybody in general to the Jews specifically. He continues by addressing the Jews directly. Verses 17–21:

**17 Behold, thou art called a Jew, and restest in the law, and makest thy boast of God, 18 And knowest his will, and approvest the things that are more excellent, being instructed out of the law; 19 And art confident that thou thyself art a**

guide of the blind, a light of them which are in darkness, 20 An instructor of the foolish, a teacher of babes, which hast the form of knowledge and of the truth in the law. 21 Thou therefore which teachest another, teachest thou not thyself? thou that preachest a man should not steal, dost thou steal?

Paul is exposing the hypocrisy of many of the religious Jews of that day. In Luke 18, we previously discussed the Pharisees.

We continue. Romans 2:22–24:

22 Thou that sayest a man should not commit adultery, dost thou commit adultery? thou that abhorrest idols, dost thou commit sacrilege? 23 Thou that makest thy boast of the law, through breaking the law dishonourest thou God? 24 For the name of God is blasphemed among the Gentiles through you, as it is written.

Where is this written? The prophet Nathan confronts King David concerning his sinful behavior. 2 Samuel 12:9:

**9** Wherefore hast thou despised the commandment of the LORD, to do evil in his sight? thou hast killed Uriah the Hittite with the sword, and hast taken his wife to be thy wife, and hast slain him with the sword of the children of Ammon.

David acknowledges his sin to Nathan. God has put aside David's sin, but there are consequences. Drop down to verses 13–14:

**13** And David said unto Nathan, I have sinned against the LORD. And Nathan said unto David, The LORD also hath put away thy sin; thou shalt not die. **14** Howbeit, because by this deed thou hast given great occasion to the enemies of the LORD to blaspheme, the child also that is born unto thee shall surely die.

The enemies of the Lord would be the Gentiles or the non-Jews. For this reason, it was written in Scripture, "for the name of God is blasphemed among the Gentiles through you." The *you* would be the Jews. This is just one example from the Old Testament to which Paul refers. It was because of the hypocrisy of the Jews that the Gentiles blasphemed God.

Let us return to Romans 2:25–27:

**25 For circumcision verily profit-eth, if thou keep the law: but if thou be a breaker of the law, thy circumcision is made uncircumcision. 26 Therefore if the uncircumcision keep the righteousness of the law, shall not his uncircumcision be counted for circumcision? 27 And shall not uncircumcision which is by nature, if it fulfil the law, judge thee, who by the letter and circumcision dost transgress the law?**

When we talk about keeping the Law, are we talking about sinless perfection? Are we talking about being an observer of the Law according to what the Law says? As we know, the Law had a system of sacrifices included as part of the Law for the purpose of dealing with sin. When Israel would sin, they would offer the required sin offerings to cover the sins they had committed. However, what God was looking for from Israel was faith in what God had said. We cannot be made righteous by the Law because people continually break God's Law. However, observing the Law with a heart of faith is different. That is the response God was seeking from Israel.

Here is an example. Luke 1: 5–6:

**5 There was in the days of Herod, the king of Judaea, a certain priest named Zacharias, of the course of Abia: and his wife was of the daughters of Aaron, and her name was Elisabeth. 6 And they were both righteous before God, walking in all the commandments and ordinances of the Lord blameless.**

Luke, inspired by the Holy Spirit, writes that Zacharias and his wife Elizabeth "were both righteous before God." One could ask, "How can this be? No one has kept the Law perfectly except the Lord Jesus Christ." Paul is not talking about sinlessness. He is not saying that Zacharias and Elizabeth were sinless. He is saying that when they did sin, they followed the instructions of the Law based upon their faith in what God had said. They did it by faith; not with a heart of self-righteousness, like the Pharisees. They understood that, as sinners, they needed God's mercy. Therefore, because of their faith, God declared them righteous.

We continue. Romans 2:28:

**28 For he is not a Jew, which is one outwardly; neither is that circumcision, which is outward in the flesh:**

The Jews, particularly the Pharisees, held the position they were in a right standing with God. First, they believed they were privileged because they were the seed of Abraham. Second, they thought they were righteous in themselves by observing the Law. However, they did not observe the Law through faith, rather they made up new rules, regulations, and traditions. By doing so, they could circumvent what the Law actually taught. They became righteous in themselves. They declared themselves to be righteous because they were keep ing certain rules and regulations which they had made up themselves. Paul writes, "he is not a Jew, which is one outwardly." He continues, "neither is circumcision that which is done outwardly in the flesh." His point is that it is their hearts that need to be circumcised figuratively or spiritually; not the physical circumcision. Circumcision done by hands was just a token or an outward sign of the covenant God made with Abraham. However, it was their hearts that needed to be circumcised.

Here is something I would like you to see. John 8:32–33:

> **32 And ye shall know the truth, and the truth shall make you free. 33 They answered him, We be Abraham's seed, and were never in bondage to any man:**

**how sayest thou, Ye shall be made free?**

See, right from the start of His ministry, they challenged Jesus' words because they had no spiritual understanding in their hearts. They did not understand what the Lord was saying to them. It was all about the physical and nothing about the spiritual. Verses 34–37:

> 34 Jesus answered them, Verily, verily, I say unto you, Whosoever committeth sin is the servant of sin. 35 And the servant abideth not in the house for ever: but the Son abideth ever. 36 If the Son therefore shall make you free, ye shall be free indeed. 37 I know that ye are Abraham's seed; but ye seek to kill me, because my word hath no place in you.

Concerning the phrase "my word has no place in you," Jesus was speaking about their heart. It was hardened. Their hearts were uncircumcised.

John continues. Verse 38:

> 38 I speak that which I have seen with my Father: and ye do that which ye have seen with your father.

When Jesus used the words *your father*, He was referring to the Devil, the father of lies. We will finish this thought. Verses 39–45:

> 39 They answered and said unto him, Abraham is our father. Jesus saith unto them, If ye were Abraham's children, ye would do the works of Abraham. 40 But now ye seek to kill me, a man that hath told you the truth, which I have heard of God: this did not Abraham. 41 Ye do the deeds of your father. Then said they to him, We be not born of fornication; we have one Father, even God.
>
> 42 Jesus said unto them, If God were your Father, ye would love me: for I proceeded forth and came from God; neither came I of myself, but he sent me. 43 Why do ye not understand my speech? even because ye cannot hear my word. 44 Ye are of your father the devil, and the lusts of your father ye will do. He was a murderer from the beginning, and abode not in the truth, because there is no truth in him. When he speaketh a lie, he speaketh of his own: for he is a liar, and the father of it. 45 And because I tell you the truth, ye believe me not.

Everything concerning the religious Jews was outwardly in the flesh which is in the physical. They had no spiritual understanding.

After the crucifixion, this did not change. Stephen, the first martyr, is about to be stoned to death by the religious leaders of Israel. For what cause was he to be stoned? Acts 7. 51–54:

> 51 **Ye stiffnecked and uncircumcised in heart and ears, ye do always resist the Holy Ghost: as your fathers did, so do ye. 52 Which of the prophets have not your fathers persecuted? and they have slain them which shewed before of the coming of the Just One; of whom ye have been now the betrayers and murderers: 53 Who have received the law by the disposition of angels, and have not kept it. 54 When they heard these things, they were cut to the heart, and they gnashed on him with their teeth.**

Stephen, inspired by the Holy Spirit, correctly accuses them of being "stiff-necked and uncircumcised in heart and ears."

The above is what Paul was dealing with concerning the Jews when he writes, "for he is not a Jew which is one outwardly; neither is circumcision which is something done only outwardly in the flesh." Romans 2:29:

**29 But he is a Jew, which is one inwardly; and circumcision is that of the heart, in the spirit, and not in the letter; whose praise is not of men, but of God.**

Many Christians misuse the above verse to say something it does not. They say we need to become believers in Christ. They will use terms like born-again and say we must receive Jesus into our heart. Finally, they try to convince us that when someone becomes a believer, they are spiritual Jews. That is not the case at all.

Christians, those saved by the Gospel of Grace, will never become "spiritual" Jews. Paul is directing these verses to the Jews. It is the Jews who are the beneficiaries of the covenant promises made to their fathers: Abraham, Isaac, and Jacob. Their inheritance is earthly. The promises God made to the Jews will be fulfilled upon the earth at the return of their Messiah. However, those who accept the Gospel of Grace are part of the Body of Christ. Their inheritance is heavenly. In Paul's epistle to the Grace Believers in Ephesus, he writes, "that ye may know what is the hope of his calling, and what the riches of the glory of his inheritance in the saints" (Eph. 1:18).

# 4

# Romans 3 (Part I)

In the previous chapter, Paul said, "he is a Jew who is one inwardly; whose circumcision is of the heart and the spirit and not according to the letter of the Law." Paul begins by asking a question. Romans 3:1:

**1 What advantage then hath the Jew? or what profit is there of circumcision?**

Is there any advantage to being a Jew? They have one advantage over the Gentile. They received God's Law and His revelations. In other words, all the prophets, kings, poets, and historical chronicles were received by the Jews. They are the custodians of the Word of God.

Paul answers his question. Verse 2:

**2 Much every way: chiefly, because that unto them were committed the oracles of God.**

The oracles of God were given to the prophets of Israel, meticulously copied by hand, and preserved. That is one advantage the Jews have. Another advantage is that they are from the seed of Abraham. In Genesis 12, God made a covenant with Abraham. God told him that in his seed all the nations of the earth would be blessed. Salvation for the Jews is part of the prophetic program. Salvation will be available to the Gentiles through Israel. In fact, after the Dispensation of Grace comes to a close, salvation for the Gentiles will only be available through Israel after the Rapture.

Consider the Samaritan woman who encountered the Lord at Jacob's well. Samaritans were viewed as a mixed race being both Jew and Gentile. Therefore, the religious leaders did not believe they were worthy of recognition. Yet, the Lord spoke to this woman. John 4:22:

**22 Ye worship ye know not what: we know what we worship: for salvation is of the Jews.**

Again, prior to the Dispensation of Grace, if Gentiles

wanted salvation from God, they had to go through Israel. This will also be true after the close of the Dispensation of Grace. It is for that reason that God chose Israel. He gave them the Law and all the revelation through their prophets.

Let us move on. Romans 3:3:

**3 For what if some did not believe? shall their unbelief make the faith of God without effect?**

What Paul is saying here is very important. He is saying that if the Jews do not believe, it does not change the truth of God's Word. God's Word never changes. Their unbelief, their lack of faith, does not make the faith of God ineffective. God will still do what He said He will do. That is what Paul means by *the faith of God*. The *faith of God* is God's faithfulness and that will never change. It does not matter if all of Israel does not believe. It does not matter because the truths that God gave to Israel will never change. If some do not believe, then it does not affect *the faith of God*. Their unbelief does not change God's truth. Verse 4:

**4 God forbid: yea, let God be true, but every man a liar; as it is written, That thou mightest be justified in thy say**

**ings, and mightest overcome when thou art judged.**

Many Bible students find this verse a little hard to understand. It sounds as if God needs to be justified. Does God need to defend His actions or judgments?

Let us turn to Psalms 51:1–4:

**1 Have mercy upon me, O God, according to thy lovingkindness: according unto the multitude of thy tender mercies blot out my transgressions. 2 Wash me throughly from mine iniquity, and cleanse me from my sin. 3 For I acknowledge my transgressions: and my sin is ever before me. 4 Against thee, thee only, have I sinned, and done this evil in thy sight: that thou mightest be justified when thou speakest, and be clear when thou judgest.**

Notice the psalmist said that God "might be justified" when He speaks and be clear when He judges. Paul is quoting what King David wrote in this psalm. God will always be true to what He said He will do. God will be justified in his sayings and He will overcome when He is judged by man. Sinful man is arrogant, prideful and boastful. He will criticize God, judge Him, and question all that God is doing. However, God will always prove Himself to be true.

Consider the Lord's words concerning John the Baptist. Luke 7:24–30:

> 24 And when the messengers of John were departed, he began to speak unto the people concerning John, What went ye out into the wilderness for to see? A reed shaken with the wind? 25 But what went ye out for to see? A man clothed in soft raiment? Behold, they which are gorgeously apparelled, and live delicately, are in kings' courts. 26 But what went ye out for to see? A prophet? Yea, I say unto you, and much more than a prophet.

> 27 This is he, of whom it is written, Behold, I send my messenger before thy face, which shall prepare thy way before thee. 28 For I say unto you, Among those that are born of women there is not a greater prophet than John the Baptist: but he that is least in the kingdom of God is greater than he. 29 And all the people that heard him, and the publicans, justified God, being baptized

**with the baptism of John.** 30 **But the Pharisees and lawyers rejected the counsel of God against themselves, being not baptized of him.**

Luke tells us that all the people that heard Jesus, including the publicans, "justified" God, having been baptized by John the Baptist. Let us compare their reaction to that of the Pharisees. They "rejected the counsel of God against themselves" because they had not been baptized by John. They heard but did not believe.

Those who believed justify God. How do they justify God? Well, just like what King David said in Psalm 51, they are agreeing with God. They agree or accept that God is going to do what He said He would do. They believe that God's words are true. In other words, they are agreeing with God, that God is right, and what God says is true. They proved this by being baptized by John the Baptist. This was evidence that they believed what he was preaching was from God. It was evidence that what the Lord Jesus Christ was saying to Israel was true. However, the Pharisees rejected the words of God against themselves because they did not believe and were not baptized. In other words, they proved that they were rejecting what God was saying to them. Being critical of what God was saying, they were passing judgment on God.

The key points Paul is making is that God will have the final word and He will be justified in every respect. His word is true. He is faithful to do all that He said He will do. Romans 3:5-6:

> **5 But if our unrighteousness commend the righteousness of God, what shall we say? Is God unrighteous who taketh vengeance? (I speak as a man) 6 God forbid: for then how shall God judge the world?**

This is just the kind of question a lost man would ask, right? No, it is not acceptable to be unrighteous in order to make God appear more righteous. That is ridiculous. If everything God says is true, why would it make God unrighteous when He takes vengeance against those who are unrighteous,? It is His truth that justifies His actions. It is a self-righteous and sinful man who wants to judge the God that judges the world. Man will fail because everything that God does is based solely upon Truth.

Paul continues his argument by speaking as a sinful man himself. Verse 7:

**7 For if the truth of God hath more abounded through my lie unto his glory; why yet am I also judged as a sinner?**

This question twists the facts in the same way prideful Man thinks. In his fallacy, Man contends that his sinning somehow benefits God and, therefore, he asks why he is still judged as a sinner. Paul continues this hypothetical argument. Verse 8:

**8 And not rather, (as we be slanderously reported, and as some affirm that we say,) Let us do evil, that good may come? whose damnation is just.**

Such is the thinking of a lost man, someone with a reprobate mind. Verse 9:

**9 What then? are we better than they? No, in no wise: for we have before proved both Jews and Gentiles, that they are all under sin;**

Man will always seek to justify himself in some way. He will take things that God has said and twist them, but God is a righteous God. Everything that is wrong and everything that is unrighteous He will judge. For those who are under God's grace, that judgment was put upon His Son the Lord Jesus Christ at the Cross. That is why we can say we are righteous. Why? It is because God's righteousness has been imputed to us as a free gift through our faith. Our faith is believing in what Christ did for us on the Cross. We are justified because all our penalties for sin were paid in full. God put our just punishment for our sins upon His Son.

We continue. Verses 10–11:

**10 As it is written, There is none righteous, no, not one: 11 There is none that understandeth, there is none that seeketh after God.**

When Paul speaks about no one being righteous, he is excluding Jesus Christ Who is righteous. Even if someone were able to live a righteous life without sin, they would still have to contend with Adam's original sin. Christ was born from of virgin and led a sinless life. He was the Son of God through a human mother. Therefore, He is excluded from corruption by Adam's original sin. There were people that did seek after righteousness as we find them in the Old Testament. Abraham sought after righteousness. David sought after righteousness. Yes, they sought righteousness, but it was God's righteousness that they sought. They believed God and it was believing

God that was their source of righteousness. It was not something they achieved on their own. This goes back to Romans 1. People had gotten to a point in history where they chose not to retain God in their knowledge. As a result, they have no understanding and no longer seek after God.

We now know one of the most important things when it comes to revealing the truth to people. When sharing the gospel with others, we need to realize that some people may never have heard this before. It is like confronting someone with the truth when they are not seeking the truth. Luke recorded the speech that the Apostle Paul gave at Mars' Hill in Ephesus. Acts 17:22–23:

> 22 **Then Paul stood in the midst of Mars' hill, and said, Ye men of Athens, I perceive that in all things ye are too superstitious.** 23 **For as I passed by, and beheld your devotions, I found an altar with this inscription, TO THE UNKNOWN GOD. Whom therefore ye ignorantly worship, him declare I unto you.**

The citizens in Ephesus chose to seek the true God, even though they did not know Him. Verses 24–29:

24 God that made the world and all things therein, seeing that he is Lord of heaven and earth, dwelleth not in temples made with hands; 25 Neither is worshipped with men's hands, as though he needed anything, seeing he giveth to all life, and breath, and all things; 26 And hath made of one blood all nations of men for to dwell on all the face of the earth, and hath determined the times before appointed, and the bounds of their habitation;

27 That they should seek the Lord, if haply they might feel after him, and find him, though he be not far from every one of us: 28 For in him we live, and move, and have our being; as certain also of your own poets have said, For we are also his offspring. 29 Forasmuch then as we are the offspring of God, we ought not to think that the Godhead is like unto gold, or silver, or stone, graven by art and man's device.

Notice what Paul is doing. He is giving these people information that they need in order to understand and know God. That is what we need to do when we give somebody the Gospel of Grace.

He continues. Verses 30–31:

**30 And the times of this ignorance God winked at; but now commandeth all men every where to repent: 31 Because he hath appointed a day, in the which he will judge the world in righteousness by that man whom he hath ordained; whereof he hath given assurance unto all men, in that he hath raised him from the dead.**

There were times in the past when God winked, or overlooked, man's ignorance of who the Lord Jesus Christ is. That was in the past. He continues with his speech but it denotes a change from the past to the present. Now, God commands all men everywhere to repent which means to change their minds. Why? It is because He has appointed a day in which He will judge the world. He will judge the world in righteousness which is only available through His Son.

God has appointed His Son to be Judge over all. The only righteousness that will stand before God is the righteousness of Christ. How can we be sure that Christ's righteousness is enough? God has given assurance to all men that it was because of Christ's righteousness that He raised Christ from the dead. That is sufficient proof according to God. The

Ephesians were seeking God even though they did not know God. Paul starts by showing them they can know God. How? They can have a relationship with God through His Son Lord Jesus Christ.

Paul makes the point that no one understands. No one is seeking after God. All people have chosen to turn away from God and the truth. We return to Romans 3:12:

> 12 **They are all gone out of the way, they are together become unprofitable; there is none that doeth good, no, not one.**

He goes on to describe people who have rejected God by putting God far from their minds. The list of their attributes is not pretty; even frightening. This is evident as we look around at our present circumstances today. When Paul finishes the list, he comes to the conclusion that no one fears God. Verses 13–18:

> 13 **Their throat is an open sepulchre; with their tongues they have used deceit; the poison of asps is under their lips: 14 Whose mouth is full of cursing and bitterness: 15 Their feet are swift to shed blood: 16 Destruction and misery are in their ways: 17 And the way of peace have they not known: 18 There is**

**no fear of God before their eyes.**

Here, the word *fear* means *respect*. They have no *respect* for God.

Paul is talking about all people. This includes both Jews and Gentiles. It is a global problem. Although the Jews had God's Law and the Prophets, they rejected God's Word. Instead, they went their own way by making up their own rules and regulations. They had lost their faith. Verse 19:

> 19 **Now we know that what things soever the law saith, it saith to them who are under the law: that every mouth may be stopped, and all the world may become guilty before God.**

All the world is under the Law. The Jews are under the Mosaic Law. The non-Jews or Gentiles are under the Law of Conscience which is also known as the Moral Law. If we do not have the righteousness of the Lord Jesus Christ imputed to us, then we will be judged by the applicable Law. Again, whether Jew or Gentile, it is clear that *all* the world is guilty before God. Why? It is because the Law condemns everyone. Paul reaches a conclusion. Verse 20:

> 20 **Therefore by the deeds of the law**

**there shall no flesh be justified in his sight: for by the law is the knowledge of sin.**

The only purpose for the Law is to show everyone two things. First, they are sinners. Second, they are in need of salvation.

We will continue with the remainder of Romans 3 in the next chapter.

# 5

## Romans 3 (Part II)

We will continue with Romans 3:21–23:

**21 But now the righteousness of God without the law is manifested, being witnessed by the law and the prophets; 22 Even the righteousness of God which is <u>by faith of Jesus Christ</u> unto all and upon all them that believe: for there is no difference: 23 For all have sinned, and come short of the glory of God;**

Paul explains that the righteousness of God comes by the "faith of Jesus Christ." It is important to notice that Paul states that righteousness comes by the faith "of" Jesus Christ. This is not the same thing as faith "in" Jesus Christ." What is the difference?

We must understand that Paul is talking about

"righteousness" and not "salvation." We receive our salvation by having faith in the finished work of Christ. He did everything to secure salvation. However, as the Body of Christ, the righteousness we receive is not our own. We do not earn our righteousness by merit, through works, or by keeping the Law. Only Christ alone is righteous. The faith "of" Christ has to do with His *faithfulness* to the Father. He accomplished everything necessary for salvation – for both Jews and Gentiles.

Therefore, salvation can only be obtained through Jesus Christ. His death, burial, and resurrection provided the final solution for sin. Again, it makes no difference whether you are a Jew or Gentile. However, it will apply to each of them differently. For those who accept the Gospel of Grace by faith, salvation is received immediately. However, for the Jews saved by the Gospel of the Kingdom, their salvation will be received when their Messiah returns. They must acknowledge that Jesus is their Messiah and the Son of God. They must repent and be baptized. They must obey the Law and contin- ue to show their faith by good works. Should they do this and endure to the end, they will receive their salvation at the end of the Tribulation. (See Matthew 24.)

Let us continue Romans 3:24:

**24 Being justified freely by his grace through the redemption that is in Christ Jesus:**

Let us carefully consider the phrase "being justified freely." The word *justify* means *to remove guilt, be made righteous* or *declared not guilty*. The word *freely* means *without conditions* or *with no stipulations*. As members of the Body of Christ, we are "justified freely." Should someone ask, "What's the catch?" We can confidently respond, "Nothing!" Our justification is undeserved. It is unmerited and unearned. It is a gift! We are justified freely because of what Christ did for us on the Cross. We did not merit this justification in any way, shape, or form. It is solely based upon what Jesus has done. It has nothing to do with what we have done or will do. That is what *freely* means. It is "free." No strings or conditions are attached. That, my friends, is *grace!*

How is this possible? It is only possible because Christ paid the price in full. For that reason, it is free to all who will accept His gift by faith. Here we are referring to the Gospel of Grace. Verse 25:

**25 Whom God hath set forth to be a propitiation through faith in his blood, to**

**declare his righteousness for the remission of sins that are past, through the forbearance of God;**

The Law requires punishment for sin. The word *propitiation* means *a payment that fully satisfies the justice of God.* Sin must be punished because God is a holy God. He is a just God. As such, any violation of His Law is sin and sin must be punished. His sacrifice is sufficient for all. He took our punishment upon the Cross for all the wrongs we have done or will ever do. It was dealt with once and for all at the Cross through "His blood." It is by faith alone and grace alone. I feel I am hammering this point home. I like to say, "By grace through faith plus nothing!"

We continue. Verse 26:

**26 To declare, I say, at this time his righteousness: that he might be just, and the justifier of him which believeth in Jesus.**

Here, Paul is declaring the righteousness of Christ Who is both the Just as well as the Justifier of those who believe. He uses the words "at this time." There is a dispensational time change here. We discussed the fact there are two applications to what the Lord Jesus Christ did on the Cross. Concerning the Grace

Believers, their past, present, and future sins have been paid for by the blood of Jesus Christ. In verse 25, Paul writes about "the forbearance of God." Although Grace Believers may sin, God will forbear punishment because of His Son's righteousness.

Christ's sacrifice applies differently for Israel. Their sins will be held in remission until the Messiah returns. Peter declares this to the Jews at Pentecost, "Repent, and be baptized every one of you in the name of Jesus Christ for the remission of sins" (Acts 2:38). When we think of cancer, *remission* means that the cancer is *no longer active or growing* even though it still may exist. To be saved under the Kingdom Gospel, Jews must have faith that Jesus Christ is their Messiah and the Son of God. He presently is acting as their High Priest. (See Hebrews 3.) Their sins are in remission being held on account until they are settled at the return of their Messiah.

Let us look at Hebrews. This is a wonderful book that explains the priesthood of Jesus Christ on behalf of the Jews. It is superior to the Levitical system of sacrifices under the Mosaic Law. That system pointed to the coming Christ. Now, He is both Israel's Sacrifice and presently acting as their eternal High Priest. Hebrews 9:22:

**22** And almost all things are by the law purged with blood; and without shedding of blood is no remission.

God gave Israel the Law and the sacrificial system. However, those animal sacrifices could only temporarily cover their sins. They could not remove them. It was a representation, a picture, or a type, of the one true blood Sacrifice that they needed. The Law and its system of sacrifices were designed to teach Israel about their need, but they did not understand. However, the fact still remains that "without shedding of blood is no remission."

It is important to understand that Hebrews was written to the Jews. Therefore, the "us" in the last verse refers to those saved by the Kingdom Gospel. Verses 23–24:

**23** It was therefore necessary that the patterns of things in the heavens should be purified with these; but the heavenly things themselves with better sacrifices than these. **24** For Christ is not entered into the holy places made with hands, which are the figures of the true; but into heaven itself, now to appear in the presence of God for us:

The words "holy places made with hands" refer to the physical tabernacles made on the earth by men. It is no longer about a human priest going into the tabernacle on earth anymore. That was only a temporary picture of something permanent to come. The Book of Hebrews was written to Israel. The Body of Christ has no need for intercession. Our sins were justified and we have been declared "not guilty."

We continue. Verses 25–26:

> 25 **Nor yet that he should offer himself often, as the high priest entereth into the holy place every year with blood of others; 26 For then must he often have suffered since the foundation of the world: but now once in the end of the world hath he appeared to put away sin by the sacrifice of himself.**

The words "the end of the world" refer to the end of the age which completes  the Dispensation of Law. At that point, the[DG1] Kingdom will be established and the Final Judgment will be imminent. Presently, Jesus Christ is their Tabernacle, their Sacrifice, and their High Priest. Christ is all three . . . in One!

Remaining in Hebrews, this still pertains to the Jews. Verses 27–28:

**27 And as it is appointed unto men once to die, but after this the judgment: 28 So Christ was once offered to bear the sins of many; and unto them that look for him shall he appear the second time without sin unto salvation.**

Notice that it says, "the sins of many" and does not say "the sins of all." This concerns Israel. Believing Israel will have their sins placed in remission. However. their sins will not be forgiven until His Coming. However, not all Israel will have their sins forgiven. Their salvation is contingent upon their faith which must be constantly proven by good works. Kingdom Believers must continue to exhibit an active faith. Look again at the verse above. Jesus "will bear the sins of many," but not all. When their Messiah returns, those who continued in faith will have their sins blotted out.

We saw Peter's instruction to those at the Feast of Pentecost who desired to be saved. Here, Peter confirms the above. Acts 3:19-21:

**19 Repent ye therefore, and be converted, that your sins may be blotted out, when the times of refreshing shall come from the presence of the Lord; 20 And he shall send Jesus Christ, which**

**before was preached unto you: 21 Whom the heaven must receive until the times of restitution of all things, which God hath spoken by the mouth of all his holy prophets since the world began.**

Peter makes it clear. If they believe that Christ is their Messiah, repent, and believe He is the Son of God, then all of their past sins will be in remission. Furthermore, if they continue in their faith, then all of their sins will be blotted out when He returns to establish His Kingdom. What Peter preached to the Jews here is in full agreement with the writer of Hebrews.

Let us continue. Romans 3: 27:

**27 Where is boasting then? It is excluded. By what law? of works? Nay: but by the law of faith.**

It is all about *faith*. It is not about our works. Again, it is all about our *faith*. It is the only valid response to the Gospel of Grace that God will accept. The only thing God will accept from us is believing what Jesus did on the Cross for us. Each of us must exercise our free will and choose to *believe*. Ephesians 2: 8–9:

**8 For by grace are ye saved through**

**faith; and that not of yourselves: it is the gift of God: 9 Not of works, lest any man should boast.**

Salvation is offered as a *gift*. Nothing is expected in return. Once received, nothing is demanded to keep or maintain this gift, as some teach. This free gift of salvation is offered to everyone, but only received by those who accept the offer. Now, this is truly wonderful news! This, my friend, is the Gospel of Grace!

Paul uses the word *therefore* in the next verse as he concludes his thoughts on the subject. Romans 3:28–29:

**28 Therefore we conclude that a man is <u>justified by faith without the deeds of the law</u>. 29 Is he the God of the Jews only? is he not also of the Gentiles? Yes, of the Gentiles also:**

Paul refers to "the law of faith." This puts forth the sense of it being a principle where believing God is the basis of faith. This same "principle of believing God" dates back to Abraham who is "the father of faith."

Let us pause and consider this "principle of faith." Sometimes, the words *principle* and *law* are synonymous. This principle or doctrine can only be learned by the hearing of the Word of God. Romans 10:17:

> 17 **So then faith cometh by hearing, and hearing by the word of God.**

These last verses of the chapter are important. Romans 3:30:

> 30 **Seeing it is one God, which shall justify the circumcision by faith, and uncircumcision through faith.**

What does this mean? The word *circumcision* refers to *Israel* and the word *uncircumcision* refers to the *non-Jews or Gentiles*. Both of the two entities receive their justification because of their faith although it is applied differently.

Let us consider the words *by faith* for a moment by looking at some verses. Isaiah 53:10–12:

> 10 **Yet it pleased the LORD to bruise him; he hath put him to grief: when thou shalt make his soul an offering for sin, he shall see his seed, he shall prolong his days, and the pleasure of the LORD shall prosper in his hand. 11 He shall see of the travail of his soul, and**

**shall be satisfied: by his knowledge shall <u>my righteous servant justify many; for he shall bear their iniquities.</u> 12 Therefore will I divide him a portion with the great, and he shall divide the spoil with the strong; because he hath poured out his soul unto death: and he was numbered with the transgressors; and he bare the sin of many, and made intercession for the transgressors.**

Some of you may have deduced that this is a prophecy about the Lord Jesus Christ going to the Cross. So, when Paul says in Romans 3, *the circumcision,* which means *the Jews,* shall be justified *by faith,* he is referring to Isaiah 53. It is clear that the believing Jew will be justified *by their faith* in this Suffering Servant, their Messiah. Believing Jews understand that Isaiah 53 is foretelling: that (1) Christ is their Messiah, (2) He sacrificed Himself for the remission of their sins, and (3) He will one day blot out those sins when He returns to establish His Kingdom.

Salvation is only possible through Jesus Christ. However, it is applied differently to those saved according to the Gospel of the Kingdom and those saved according to the Gospel of Grace. Because of their past, the Jews have a tendency to have faith and lose it. Therefore, the Lord requires them to maintain their faith until the end. For this reason, James, teaching believing Jews, wrote, "But wilt thou know, O vain man, that faith without works is dead?" (Jas. 2:20). And, the writer of Hebrews wrote, "Now the just shall live by faith: but if any man draw back, my soul shall have no pleasure in him. But we are not of them who draw back unto perdition; but of them that believe to the saving of the soul" (Heb. 10:38-39). A quick study of Hebrews 11 will reveal the words "by faith" are used sixteen times as it is applied to Israel's illustrious history of their faithful. However, the Gospel of Grace saves believers by grace *through faith*. This is effective immediately upon believing and without the requirement of works as proof.

This brings us to the last verse. Romans 3:31:

**31 Do we then make void the law through faith? God forbid: yea, we establish the law.**

How does all this *establish* or *confirm* the Law? For the answer, turn to Galatians 3:24–25:

**24 Wherefore the law was our schoolmaster to bring us unto Christ, that we might be justified by faith. 25 But after that faith is come, we are no longer under a schoolmaster.**

The purpose of the Law is to show us our sinfulness. It proves that we are unable to keep it. The Law brings us to the knowledge of sin where we realize our need for a Savior. Look at Galatians 3:13–14:

> 13 **Christ hath redeemed us from the curse of the law, being made a curse for us: for it is written, Cursed is every one that hangeth on a tree: 14 That the blessing of Abraham might come on the Gentiles through Jesus Christ; that we might receive the promise of the Spirit through faith.**

Since Paul is writing to Grace Believers, notice in the last line above that he says *through faith*. The question remains, "What establishes the Law?" The work of Christ upon the Cross establishes the Law. It proves the perfection of God and the righteousness of Christ Who is perfect according to the Law. He fulfilled all the requirements of the Law for everyone. Then, He took upon Himself the required punishment for all sinners who broke the Law. Therefore, Christ established the Law when He fulfilled the Law.

# 6

## Romans 4

When we read Romans, we are learning the doctrines for salvation and for service. All of the Pauline epistles were written specifically to those saved by the Gospel of Grace called the Body of Christ. Romans is the foundation upon which all the other epistles that follow are built. Matthew, Mark, Luke, and John are a continuation of the Old Testament. The Gospels teach the Gospel of the Kingdom to the Jews. Acts provides us with an historical record of the transition from the Gospel of the Kingdom to Paul's Gospel of Grace. This book is where we get doctrinally grounded. Romans 4:1-2:

> 1 **What shall we say then that Abraham our father, as pertaining to the flesh, hath found? 2 For if Abraham were justified by works, he hath whereof to glory; but not before God.**

Why does Paul use the words "Abraham our father" in this first verse? I would like to take a look at this because I am a former Pentecostal and was, in the past, involved in the charismatic movement. They teach that if Abraham is our father, then all the blessings promised to Abraham are for the church today. However, that is not true. Therefore, what are these verses teaching? Galatians 3:6–9:

> **6 Even as Abraham believed God, and it was accounted to him for righteousness. 7 Know ye therefore that they which are of faith, the same are the children of Abraham. 8 And the scripture, foreseeing that God would justify the heathen through faith, preached before the gospel unto Abraham, saying, In thee shall all nations be blessed. 9 So then they which be of faith are blessed with faithful Abraham.**

When Paul writes "preached before the gospel unto Abraham," the word *gospel* means *good news*. However, the good news that God preached to Abraham was not the Gospel of Grace. He writes "So then they which be of faith are blessed with faithful Abraham." In the United States, George Washington is referred to as the father of their country because of his part in the founding of the United States of America.

However, the citizens are not literally children of George Washington. In Genesis, Abraham was justified *by faith*. Likewise, those who believe God *by faith* are blessed because of their faith along with Abraham. So, in a spiritual sense, Abraham is the father of those justified *by faith* alone without works. For that reason, Paul uses Abraham as an example.

We continue in Galatians. Verses 13–14:

> 13 **Christ hath redeemed us from the curse of the law, being made a curse for us: for it is written, Cursed is every one that hangeth on a tree: 14 That the blessing of Abraham might come on the Gentiles through Jesus Christ; that we might receive the promise of the Spirit through faith.**

Note the words "that the blessing of Abraham might come on the Gentiles." This is a verse many charismatics will use to say that the church now has the blessings of Israel, but that is not true. To understand Scripture, we must always follow the context. Galatians 3:11–12:

> 11 **But that no man is justified by the law in the sight of God, it is evident: for, The just shall live by faith. 12 And the**

**law is not of faith: but, The man that doeth them shall live in them.**

It is critical that we understand that the Law is not faith! I cannot overemphasize this enough.

Let us look at "the blessing of Abraham." We can see above that those who are of faith are blessed along with faithful Abraham. So, "the blessing of Abraham" is the fact that Abraham was justified *by faith alone*. He was blessed by God Who imputed righteousness to him without works. The blessing to which Paul is referring would be "the righteousness received by believing God." Paul is not saying that the Body of Christ receives all the blessings promised to Israel. That is not what he is talking about at all. Paul is talking about the promise of the Spirit through faith. We must always interpret verses based upon its context.

We are promised that if we put our faith in the fact that Jesus Christ died on the Cross for our sins, was buried, and rose again the third day, then we will receive the Spirit of God through faith. That was the issue in the Galatian church. They believed that they could not receive the Spirit and be saved without the works of the Law. The Judaizers came into their church and said, "Yes, you must believe in Jesus, but you must be circumcised. You must also observe the Law!" Paul addresses this doctrinal error. Galatians 3:1–4:

> 1 O foolish Galatians, who hath bewitched you, that ye should not obey the truth, before whose eyes Jesus Christ hath been evidently set forth, crucified among you? 2 This only would I learn of you, Received ye the Spirit by the works of the law, or by the hearing of faith? 3 Are ye so foolish? having begun in the Spirit, are ye now made perfect by the flesh? 4 Have ye suffered so many things in vain? if it be yet in vain.

Paul asks them whether they received the Spirit as the result of salvation or by "the works of the Law." Verse 5:

> 5 He therefore that ministereth to you the Spirit, and worketh miracles among you, doeth he it by the works of the law, or by the hearing of faith?

The point that Paul is making is this: they did not receive salvation through the Law. The Law has no part in our salvation. We did not receive the promise of the Spirit by keeping the Law. We received the promise of the Spirit by faith. That faith is believing the gospel that Paul preaches. That is the point! Look at the last verse of Galatians. Verse 3:29:

> **29 And if ye be Christ's, then are ye Abraham's seed, and heirs according to the promise.**

Here, again, many Pentecostals will isolate this verse and take it out of context. "See there! We are heirs of the promises of Israel!" This is another example of interpreting the verses out of context. The promise made to Grace Believers is the promise of the Spirit.

Paul writes "and if ye be Christ's, then are ye Abraham's seed." He promises to those who have faith in what God said will also be Abraham's seed. They are his descendants in a spiritual sense and not the physical seed of Abraham. Think about the Pharisees and scribes who believed that, because they alone were the physical seed of Abraham, they were in a right relationship with God. However, they were not in a right relationship with God because they did not have faith. They did not trust in God. Instead, they trusted in their own righteousness. Paul makes this point in Galatians 3: we are Abraham's seed in the spiritual sense because we are blessed with faithful Abraham. We have faith in what God offers us today in the Gospel of Grace. As such, God offers us the Spirit of God; not the promises of Israel.

Let us look at Galatians 4:1–7:

1 **Now I say, That the heir, as long as he is a child, differeth nothing from a servant, though he be lord of all; 2 But is under tutors and governors until the time appointed of the father. 3 Even so we, when we were children, were in bondage under the elements of the world: 4 But when the fulness of the time was come, God sent forth his Son, made of a woman, made under the law, 5 To redeem them that were under the law, that we might receive the adoption of sons. 6 And because ye are sons, God hath sent forth the Spirit of his Son into your hearts, crying, Abba, Father. 7 Wherefore thou art no more a servant, but a son; and if a son, then an heir of God through Christ.**

Notice the word *inheritance* above. Having the Spirit that was promised to us through faith, we are now sons of God and joint heirs with Christ. (See also Romans 8:17.)

With this information, let us return to our text. Romans 4:3–10:

3 For what saith the scripture? Abraham believed God, and it was counted unto him for righteousness. 4 Now to him that worketh is the reward not reckoned of grace, but of debt. 5 But to him that worketh not, but believeth on him that justifieth the ungodly, his faith is counted for righteousness. 6 Even as David also describeth the blessedness of the man, unto whom God imputeth righteousness without works,

7 Saying, Blessed are they whose iniquities are forgiven, and whose sins are covered. 8 Blessed is the man to whom the Lord will not impute sin. 9 Cometh this blessedness then upon the circumcision only, or upon the uncircumcision also? for we say that faith was reckoned to Abraham for righteousness. 10 How was it then reckoned? when he was in circumcision, or in uncircumcision? Not in circumcision, but in uncircumcision.

Abraham was justified before he was circumcised. Righteousness was imputed to him by God before the Abrahamic Covenant. Before God required Abraham to do works to maintain the covenant relationship, he was already confident of his salvation. Later, his covenant blessings were made dependent upon works. In his epistle to the Jews, James used this as the model for Israel. He wrote, "For as the body without the spirit is dead, so faith without works is dead also" (Jas. 2:26). Abraham, like us, was justified without works and considered to be righteous before God.

Under the Law, God requires works. However, works by themselves never save anyone. It is faith that saves; not works. Works, for Israel, were simply an expression of the faith that they had in what God had told them concerning the Law. Remember, nowhere in the Bible does it ever teach that works save. Salvation is always by faith. Verses 11–16:

> 11 **And he received the sign of circumcision, a seal of the righteousness of the faith which he had yet being uncircumcised: that he might be the father of all them that believe, though they be not circumcised; that righteousness might be imputed unto them also: 12 And the father of circumcision to them who are not of the circumcision only, but who also walk in the steps of that faith of our father Abraham, which he had being yet uncircumcised.**

13 For the promise, that he should be the heir of the world, was not to Abraham, or to his seed, through the law, but through the righteousness of faith. 14 For if they which are of the law be heirs, faith is made void, and the promise made of none effect: 15 Because the law worketh wrath: for where no law is, there is no transgression. 16 Therefore it is of faith, that it might be by grace; to the end the promise might be sure to all the seed; not to that only which is of the law, but to that also which is of the faith of Abraham; who is the father of us all,

Abraham is the father of everyone who believes "by faith alone."

Let us continue. Verses 17–18:

17 (As it is written, I have made thee a father of many nations,) before him whom he believed, even God, who quickeneth the dead, and calleth those things which be not as though they were. 18 Who against hope believed in hope, that he might become the father of many nations, according to that which was spoken, So shall thy seed be.

The Law did not play a role in God's fulfilling of His promise to Abraham. God promised to save by faith alone and, therefore, Abraham's salvation did not require the Law. In fact, the Law was given to show people that they were sinners and they needed a Savior. The only thing the Law can do is show us our sin. It does its job very well.

We continue. Verses 19–22:

> 19 **And being not weak in faith, he considered not his own body now dead, when he was about an hundred years old, neither yet the deadness of Sara's womb:** 20 **He staggered not at the promise of God through unbelief; but was strong in faith, giving glory to God;** 21 **And being fully persuaded that, what he [God] had promised, he was able also to perform.** 22 **And therefore it was imputed to him for righteousness.**

When Paul says, "being fully persuaded that, what he had promised, he was able also to perform," to what is Paul referring?

We will go to Genesis to get our answer. Genesis 17:1–5:

**1** And when Abram was ninety years old and nine, the LORD appeared to Abram, and said unto him, I am the Almighty God; walk before me, and be thou perfect. **2** And I will make my covenant between me and thee, and will multiply thee exceedingly. **3** And Abram fell on his face: and God talked with him, saying, **4** As for me, behold, my covenant is with thee, and thou shalt be a father of many nations. **5** Neither shall thy name any more be called Abram, but thy name shall be Abraham; for a father of many nations have I made thee.

Now, when we look at Romans 4:18-22, we see that Abraham did not stagger in faith. He did not falter or lose faith. However, Abraham got the idea that he needed to help God out. His wife Sarah suggested to him a way he could help God carry out His plan. We should stop and think about what that means for those saved by grace.

Look at Genesis 17:15–18:

**15** And God said unto Abraham, As for Sarai thy wife, thou shalt not call her name Sarai, but Sarah shall her name be. 16 And I will bless her, and give thee a son also of her: yea, I will bless her, and she shall be a mother of nations; kings of people shall be of her. 17 Then Abraham fell upon his face, and laughed, and said in his heart, Shall a child be born unto him that is an hundred years old? and shall Sarah, that is ninety years old, bear? 18 And Abraham said unto God, O that Ishmael might live before thee!

Now, take a look at Genesis 16:1–2:

1 Now Sarai Abram's wife bare him no children: and she had an handmaid, an Egyptian, whose name was Hagar. 2 And Sarai said unto Abram, Behold now, the LORD hath restrained me from bearing: I pray thee, go in unto my maid; it may be that I may obtain children by her. And Abram hearkened to the voice of Sarai.

Abraham and Sarah knew that God had promised that from His seed there would be many nations. They did not understand that God was going to make it happen miraculously. They decided to take it upon themselves to make it happen. That is what a lot of Christians do. They think that God needs their help. We are impatient and say, "I'm going to help God make this happen." Abraham did just that. He tried to make God's promises happen through a work of the flesh. He later discovered that God was going to do it all for him.

Can you see the similarity here? Compare Abraham's faith in God's promise to him with our faith in God's promise to us. Our salvation is based our faith in God's finished work of Christ on the Cross. With Abraham's son Isaac, God did it all just as He promised. Likewise, God will complete what He promised us through the Gospel of Grace. It is for this reason that Paul compares our promise with Abraham's promise. Romans 4:20–21:

> **20 He staggered not at the promise of God through unbelief; but was strong in faith, giving glory to God; 21 And being fully persuaded that, what he had promised, he was able also to perform.**

Remember, Abraham did not stagger, or falter, at the promise of God. We read that he was "fully persuaded" that God Himself would fulfill His promise. At one point, he did think that he had to help God out. This is a good lesson for us today. Abraham was fully persuaded that what He had promised, He would perform. That was a very important lesson for the Jews as well. What Paul is saying is that Abraham trusted God, he believed God, and he had faith in God's Word.

After Abraham made the mistake with Hagar, he produced a child by the flesh. He realized that both he and Sarah needed to trust God. God was going to do everything necessary to fulfill His promise to Abraham. That is exactly what we need to do today. We need to trust God. We need to believe that He has done everything necessary for our salvation. We are already complete in Him. We cannot make ourselves any more complete in Him than we already are. He has already done that for us. Many Christians are trying to make themselves complete in God when, in fact, they are already complete in Him. Colossians 2:10–12:

> 10 **And ye are complete in him, which is the head of all principality and power: 11 In whom also ye are circumcised with the circumcision made without hands, in putting off the body of the sins of the flesh by the circumcision of Christ: 12 Buried with him in baptism, wherein also ye are risen with him through the faith of the operation of God, who hath raised him from the dead.**

With this information, we can now move on. Romans 4:23–25:

> 23 Now it was not written for his sake alone, that it was imputed to him; 24 But for us also, to whom it shall be imputed, if we believe on him that raised up Jesus our Lord from the dead; 25 Who was delivered for our offences, and was raised again for our justification.

Here is another great lesson for us. With Abraham's faith, he trusted God for everything and did not trust in his own works done in his flesh. In the last verse, Paul writes about the Lord Jesus Christ Who "was delivered for our offenses and was raised again for our justification." What does Paul mean by this?

Let us go back to Romans 1:4:

> 4 And declared to be the Son of God with power, according to the spirit of holiness, by the resurrection from the dead:

In other words, the resurrection of Christ proves that He is the Son of God Who declares Him to be so by the power of the resurrection. Christ was righteous; without sin. Yet He willingly took our place on the

Cross and suffered death on our behalf. However, because He was righteous, death could not hold Him. He is the first begotten Son of God, raised with all authority and power, because He was the first to rise from the dead.

In the Gospel of Matthew, Jesus meets with His Disciples after His resurrection. Matthew 28:18:

> 18 **And Jesus came and spake unto them, saying, <u>All power is given unto me in heaven and in earth.</u>**

Christ is referring to His position after the resurrection. So, at His resurrection, Christ was given all power "in heaven and in earth." The Apostle John records the Lord appearing to him in Revelation 1:18:

> 18 **I am he that liveth, and was dead; and, behold, I am alive for evermore, Amen; and have the keys of hell and of death.**

The Lord Jesus was raised from the dead and declared to be the Son of God with all power. Christ was given all power and authority in heaven and earth. He holds the keys of hell and death. Therefore, it is Christ Who decides. He has the keys of judgment for life and death. As we know, if someone has the keys to something, they can decide who goes in and who goes out the door. Christ is both the Just and the Justifier of those who believe. Christ is now the One Who is just. He is the One with all power and all authority. It was because of Christ's righteousness and God's acceptance of His perfect sacrifice that God raised Him from the dead. Therefore, Christ has the authority to justify us. As the Judge, He can declare us as "not guilty."

How important is it that we believe in the resurrection of Christ for our salvation? The following verses encapsulate the Gospel of Grace. Notice that Paul refers to it as *my* gospel. 1 Corinthians 15:1–2:

> 1 **Moreover, brethren, I declare un- to you <u>the gospel</u> which I preached unto you, which also ye have received, and wherein ye stand; 2 <u>By which also ye are saved</u>, if ye keep in memory what I preached unto you, unless ye have believed in vain.**

Notice, particularly, verses 3-4:

> 3 **For I delivered unto you first of all that which I also received, how that [1]Christ died for our sins according to the scriptures; 4 And that [2] he was buried, and that [3] he rose again the third**

**day according to the scriptures:**

Can you see the simplicity of the Gospel of Grace? I added numbers so you can see the three parts. It is amazing how people have tried to complicate this simple message. Like Abraham, if we believe in and have faith in God's Word, we will be saved by grace *through faith* without works. Christ has done it all.

Writing to the Ephesians, Paul confirms the simple components of salvation by the Gospel of Grace. Each Grace Believer should memorize the following verses. Ephesians 2:8-9:

> 8 For <u>by grace</u> are ye saved <u>through faith</u>; and that not of yourselves: <u>it is the gift of God</u>: 9 <u>Not of works</u>, lest any man should boast.

# 7

## Romans 5 (Part I)

In Romans 4, Paul established that our justification is *through faith* alone. He begins Romans 5 by making the following conclusion. Romans 5:1–2:

> 1 **Therefore being justified by faith, we have peace with God through our Lord Jesus Christ: 2 By whom also we have access by faith into this grace wherein we stand, and rejoice in hope of the glory of God.**

What do we have as a result of being justified by faith? First, we have peace with God. We are no longer His enemy. Second, we have been reconciled to God by the death of the Lord Jesus Christ and saved by His life. In Romans 5, Paul will work on presenting a theme.

Let us jump ahead a bit and look at some other verses supporting his points. Romans 5:10:

> 10 **For if, when we were enemies, we were reconciled to God by the death of his Son, much more, being reconciled, we shall be saved by his life.**

Compare this to Ephesians 1:6:

> 6 **To the praise of the glory of his grace, wherein he hath made us accepted in the beloved.**

Now, compare it to Colossians 1:20–22:

> 20 **And, having made peace through the blood of his cross, by him to reconcile all things unto himself; by him, I say, whether they be things in earth, or things in heaven. 21 And you, that were sometime alienated and enemies in your mind by wicked works, yet now hath he reconciled 22 In the body of his flesh through death, to present you holy and unblameable and unreproveable in his sight:**

We see a cohesive theme here. Another reference for our consideration is 2 Corinthians 5:17–19:

> 17 Therefore if any man be in Christ, he is a new creature: old things are passed away; behold, all things are become new. 18 And all things are of God, who hath reconciled us to himself by Jesus Christ, and hath given to us the ministry of reconciliation; 19 To wit, that God was in Christ, reconciling the world unto himself, not imputing their trespasses unto them; and hath committed unto us the word of reconciliation.

When Paul writes "reconciling the world unto Himself," he is not saying that Christ has saved everybody in the world. God's grace is *sufficient* for all, but only *efficient*, or *effective*, for those who choose to accept His offer. Only they will be reconciled to God. What this passage is talking about is the fact that God has provided a means of reconciliation for the whole world through the Cross, but we must have faith in His work. 2 Corinthians:20–21:

> 20 Now then we are ambassadors for Christ, as though God did beseech you by us: we pray you in Christ's stead, be ye reconciled to God. 21 For he hath made him to be sin for us, who knew no

**sin; that we might be made the right-eousness of God in him.**

Know this: when we choose to believe the gospel that the Apostle Paul preached, we are no longer God's enemy. They are presently reconciled to God *through faith*. Paul began this conclusion. Romans 5:1-2:

**1 Therefore being justified by faith, we have peace with God through our Lord Jesus Christ: 2 By whom also we have access by faith into this grace wherein we stand, and rejoice in hope of the glory of God.**

The only way we can have peace with God is to be reconciled to Him. We must believe the gospel that Paul preached: Christ died for our sins, was buried, and rose again the third day according to the Scriptures. (See 1 Corinthians 15:1–4.) Many forget the most important fact. He rose again the third day "for our justification." When we accept the gospel, we are immediately reconciled with God and have peace with Him. A lot of people will say, "I've made my peace with God." The only way to have peace with God is by accepting what God has done for them through His Son.

I would like to point out something else. This is a *positional truth.* Anyone who has believed the gospel, as far as God is concerned, has *peace with God.* It does not mean they have the *peace of God.* There is a difference. How does one attain the *peace of God?* If they trust Him, then He will give them the *peace of God* because they will no longer need to worry about death. Whether they die or are raptured, they can rest in the knowledge that they will be with Jesus forever. By applying this, my friends, we have the "peace of God."

In verse 2, the words "by Whom" refer to the Lord Jesus Christ. It is Christ Who gives us access to His grace "being fully persuaded that what God has promised, God is able to perform." This is the faith that we have in the Gospel of the Grace of God as taught by the Apostle Paul. Let us look back to Exodus when Israel had just received the Ten Commandments. Exodus 19:10–12:

> 10 **And the LORD said unto Moses, Go unto the people, and sanctify them to day and to morrow, and let them wash their clothes, 11 And be ready against the third day: for the third day the LORD will come down in the sight of all the people upon mount Sinai. 12 And thou shalt set bounds unto the people**

round about, saying, Take heed to your-selves, that ye go not up into the mount, or touch the border of it: whosoever toucheth the mount shall be surely put to death:

We continue. Exodus 20:18–19:

18 And all the people saw the thunder-ings, and the lightnings, and the noise of the trumpet, and the mountain smok-ing: and when the people saw it, they re-moved, and stood afar off. 19 And they said unto Moses, Speak thou with us, and we will hear: but let not God speak with us, lest we die.

It is interesting to note that the people of Israel could not get close to God. They could not go near the holy mountain. Only Moses was allowed to get close to Him.

Let us fast-forward to the Gospel of Matthew. Here, the angel is speaking to Mary and Joseph. Mat-thew 1:23:

23 Behold, a virgin shall be with child, and shall bring forth a son, and they shall call his name Emmanuel, which

**being interpreted is, God with us.**

At the birth of Christ, God was now with Israel in the flesh. The Lord Jesus Christ is the manifestation of God in the flesh. God was now *with* His people Israel, but He was not with the Gentiles. During His earthly ministry, Christ continued by instructing His disciples to avoid going to the Gentiles. Matthew 10:5–7:

> 5 **These twelve Jesus sent forth, and commanded them, saying, <u>Go not into the way of the Gentiles</u>, and into any city of the Samaritans enter ye not: 6 <u>But go rather to the lost sheep of the house of Israel</u>. 7 And as ye go, preach, saying, The kingdom of heaven is at hand.**

Paul confirms this in his explanation to the Gentiles concerning Israel. Romans 15:8:

> 8 **Now I say that Jesus Christ was a minister of the circumcision for the truth of God, to confirm the promises made unto the fathers:**

Here the "fathers" are Abraham, Isaac, and Jacob or Israel. During Christ's earthly ministry, He specifically came to deal with Israel. The time of the Gentiles had not yet come. I know this is very difficult for some to accept. Most people cling to what they were taught and not what the Word of God says. While Jesus was with the Jews, they rejected what He taught because it was not what they had learned from their religious leaders. Scripture is the authority when it comes to truth. Let us trust God's Word and carry on.

Jesus came to bring the good news of the Gospel of the Kingdom. Let us compare it with the Gospel of Grace. Ephesians 2:11–16:

> 11 Wherefore remember, that ye being in time past Gentiles in the flesh, who are called Uncircumcision by that which is called the Circumcision in the flesh made by hands; 12 That at that time ye were without Christ, being aliens from the commonwealth of Israel, and strangers from the covenants of promise, having no hope, and without God in the world: 13 But now in Christ Jesus ye who sometimes were far off are made nigh by the blood of Christ.
>
> 14 For he is our peace, who hath made both one, and hath broken down the middle wall of partition between us; 15 Having abolished in his flesh the

**enmity, even the law of commandments contained in ordinances; for to make in himself of twain one new man, so making peace; 16 And that he might reconcile both unto God in one body by the cross, having slain the enmity thereby:**

We should note above the phrase: "so making peace and that He might reconcile both unto God." We learn that in this current Dispensation of Grace, both Jew and Gentile can be close to God through the shed blood of Jesus Christ on the Cross. It is available to both through faith in the Gospel of Grace. We can all have access to God. Verses 17-18:

**17 And came and preached peace to you which were afar off, and to them that were nigh. 18 For through him we both have access by one Spirit unto the Father.**

Both the Jews who were *near* and the Gentiles who were *far off* now have access to God the Father through one Spirit. Faith in the Gospel of Grace grants us access through the Holy Spirit to God. By one Spirit which indwells us, and, through the Gospel of Grace wherein we stand, we are both reconciled to God.

There was a time when not even the people of Israel could get near to God. Then there was a time when God came to earth in the form of a man. God was with Israel; the Gentiles had no part in it. Now, during this Dispensation of Grace, everyone has the opportunity to accept His gracious offer of salvation. The moment we trust Christ as our Savior, we have access to God by grace through faith. If we do not believe the gospel or trust Christ as our Savior, then we do not have access to God and, therefore, we are still at enmity with Him.

If someone puts themselves under the Law for salvation, then they are no longer under grace. They are believing in another gospel. Paul wrote to the Galatians concerning this very issue. If they are not operating under grace, then they are operating under the law. One cannot do both. Our salvation is through faith in what Christ has already done for us on the Cross.

There are three basic points Paul is focusing on here at the beginning of Romans 5. First, we are justified by faith. Second, we have peace with God. Third, we can rejoice in hope of the glory of God. What does Paul mean by the "hope of the glory of God?" He is talking about the Rapture. Look at Romans 3:23:

**23 For all have sinned, and come short of the glory of God;**

We are all sinners because we have fallen short of His glory. However, if we believe the gospel, then we can rejoice in the "hope of the glory of God." This is a reference to the day when we lose our sinful corrupt bodies and our sin nature. At His Calling, we put on our glorious body like His resurrected body. We are resurrected to be with Christ in glory forever. This term, *the Rapture,* is not used in the Bible. It simply means the *catching away.*

Look at what Paul writes in Romans 8:18:

**18 For I reckon that the sufferings of this present time are not worthy to be compared with the glory which shall be revealed in us.**

When we believe the gospel, we can rejoice in "the hope of the glory of God." This is a "hope" that is sure. It is not a maybe. Like Abraham, we can be "fully persuaded that what God has promised He is able to perform." We can be confident that we will be glorified and, on that day, we will experience "the glory of God." Verse 19:

**19 For the earnest expectation of the**

creature waiteth for the manifestation
of the sons of God.

This manifestation is when we receive our glorified bodies. We are already sons of God. When we receive our glorified bodies, God has completed "the redemption of the purchased possession" (Eph. 1:14). Paul continues with the importance of hope. Verses 24–25:

> 24 For we are saved by hope: but hope that is seen is not hope: for what a man seeth, why doth he yet hope for? 25 But if we hope for that we see not, then do we with patience wait for it.

Let us go back a few verses since what we hope for is found in them. Verses 20–21:

> 20 For the creature was made subject to vanity, not willingly, but by reason of him who hath subjected the same in hope, 21 Because the creature itself also shall be delivered from the bondage of corruption into the glorious liberty of the children of God.

There it is! Our "hope of glory" is when we are brought "into the glorious liberty of the children of

God." This refers to the Rapture. We have the hope that one day we will experience "the glory of God." We will not only see the glory of God Himself, but we ourselves will also be glorified by Him on that day!

Let us return to Romans 5:3–5:

> 3 **And not only so, but we glory in trib-ulations also: knowing that tribulation worketh patience; 4 And patience, expe-rience; and experience, hope: 5 And hope mak-eth not ashamed; because the love of God is shed abroad in our hearts by the Holy Ghost which is given unto us.**

Here, the word *tribulation* means *testing*. It says we glory in testing while still in our earthly body. The word *glory* is used in the context of *rejoicing* in the same way that Paul used it in verse 2. There, he was talking about *rejoicing* in the hope of the glory of God. As difficult as it may seem, as Grace Believers, we are to rejoice in our tribulations. How is this even possible?

Allow me to give you an example from Paul's letter to the Corinthians. Paul has a personal ailment which he refers to as "a thorn in the flesh" and he sought delivery from this affliction. 2 Corinthians 12:8-9

> 8 **For this thing I besought the Lord thrice, that it might depart from me. 9 And he said unto me, My grace is sufficient for thee: for my strength is made perfect in weakness. Most gladly therefore will I rather <u>glory in my infirmities, that the power of Christ may rest upon me.</u>**

When God told Paul that His grace is sufficient and the thorn in his flesh would remain, Paul changes his attitude and says he now will glory in his infirmities. Much like our Apostle Paul who learned to glory in his infirmities, we too must glory in our infirmities or tribulations. He is not talking about the Tribulation. The Body of Christ cannot be judged for they have the righteousness of Christ. They will be removed or *caught away* before God pours out His judgment and wrath upon the world. We can be confident of this. Think about it. If Grace Believers have the righteousness of His Son, then how can God judge us? However, we must endure our testing while we remain on earth prior to the Rapture. Yet, we can rejoice in the hope of His Calling.

Let us take a moment and talk about tribulation. When Paul talks about tribulations in verse 3, he cannot be talking about the Great Tribulation. As previously mentioned, Grace Believers will not experience the wrath of God. I cannot emphasize this point enough. There are currently people on Facebook, YouTube, and other media saying that we are already in the Tribulation. In the Age of Grace, no one is experiencing the wrath of God.

Do you know why Paul begins each of his letters with a greeting that includes the words *grace* and *peace?* He is emphasizing something important. It is the fact that God is presently withholding His wrath and judgment on the world. We are living in the Age of Grace. God is withholding His wrath. They call it the Age of Grace for a reason!

Let us put this all together. Paul is saying that because of the promises God has given us we have hope! We will not be disappointed. We will not be dismayed or perplexed by circumstances. Our confidence in God's love for us will buffer us against the trials, tribulations, and difficulties of this life. Our hearts should be abundantly filled with hope of the promises God has made. This hope is the hope of *His Calling.* The Spirit is our earnest deposit assuring us of the completion of our redemption. We are "the purchased possession" (Eph. 1:14). Until then, we are not to focus on our circumstances. Instead, like Abraham, we are to hope in what God has promised knowing that He Who promised is able to perform!

In the next chapter, we will continue with Romans 5.

# 8

# Romans 5 (Part II)

So far in Romans 5, we learned that we are justified by faith and we have peace with God through Jesus Christ. We have access *through faith* to the grace wherein we stand. We also learned that we are to rejoice in the hope of *the glory of God* which is *His Calling*. We talked about how trials and tribulation bring about patience, patience brings about experience, and experience brings about hope. These three things work together in our lives so that we will not be overwhelmed or perplexed. With our confidence in God, the Spirit within us fills us with the love of God. We can go to the Word of God, read it, and understand it because of the Spirit. Finally, no matter what our circumstances are, we have the hope of glory as we await *His Calling*.

Now, let us continue. Romans 5:6–8:

**6** For when we were yet without strength, in due time Christ died for the ungodly. **7** For scarcely for a righteous man will one die: yet peradventure for a good man some would even dare to die. **8** But God commendeth his love toward us, in that, while we were yet sinners, Christ died for us.

The word *when* is an indicator of time. The phrase "when we were without strength" refers to the time when we were sinners without hope. Because of our fallen nature, we did not have the power or strength to solve this problem ourselves. Then, God offers to justify the sinner through faith in the gospel that Paul preaches. That is why he said at the beginning of the chapter that we are justified through faith and have peace with God through our Lord Jesus Christ.

Paul also experiences this lack of strength or power to prevail over sin. This emphasizes the phrase "when we were yet without strength Christ died for the ungodly." Romans 7:14–18:

**14** For we know that the law is spiritual: but I am carnal, sold under sin. **15** For that which I do I allow not: for what I would, that do I not; but what I hate, that do I. **16** If then I do that which I would not, I consent unto the law that it is good. 17 Now then it is no more I that do it, but sin that dwelleth in me. 18 For I know that in me (that is, in my flesh,) dwelleth no good thing: for to will is present with me; but how to perform that which is good I find not.

God did not bring out the good in us. Friends, there is no good in us. There is nothing good in our flesh. In fact, Paul found that he had the will or desire to do good, but he lacked the strength to do it. Verses 19–25:

19 For the good that I would I do not: but the evil which I would not, that I do. 20 Now if I do that I would not, it is no more I that do it, but sin that dwelleth in me. 21 I find then a law, that, when I would do good, evil is present with me. 22 For I delight in the law of God after the inward man: 23 But I see another law in my members, warring against the law of my mind, and bringing me into captivity to the law of sin which is in my members.

24 O wretched man that I am! who shall deliver me from the body of this death?

25 I thank God through Jesus Christ our Lord. So then with the mind I myself serve the law of God; but with the flesh the law of sin.

This concept is totally unique to Pauline doctrine. It is so important that he repeats it a- gain. Romans 8:1–4:

1 There is therefore now no condemnation to them which are in Christ Jesus, who walk not after the flesh, but after the Spirit. 2 For the law of the Spirit of life in Christ Jesus hath made me free from the law of sin and death. 3 For what the law could not do, in that it was weak through the flesh, God sending his own Son in the likeness of sinful flesh, and for sin, condemned sin in the flesh: 4 That the righteousness of the law might be fulfilled in us, who walk not after the flesh, but after the Spirit.

With that said, let us go back to Romans 5:6:

6 For when we were yet without strength, in due time Christ died for the ungodly.

It now makes complete sense. We did not have the strength or the power to keep the Law. Therefore, Christ did it for us.

It is through the Apostle Paul's Gospel of Grace that we understand what Christ's sacrifice means for us. We are going to look at three verses. Galatians 4:4:

> 4 But when the fulness of the time was come, God sent forth his Son, made of a woman, made under the law,

God had this all planned out before the foundation of the world. He knew what needed to be done and when to do it. That is the kind of God that we serve. Look at Ephesians 1:3–9:

> 3 Blessed be the God and Father of our Lord Jesus Christ, who hath blessed us with all spiritual blessings in heavenly places in Christ: 4 According as he hath chosen us in him before the foundation of the world, that we should be holy and without blame before him in love: 5 Having predestinated us unto the adoption of children by Jesus Christ to himself, according to the good pleasure of his will,

6 To the praise of the glory of his grace, wherein he hath made us accepted in the beloved. 7 In whom we have redemption through his blood, the forgiveness of sins, according to the riches of his grace; 8 Wherein he hath abounded toward us in all wisdom and prudence; 9 Having made known un- to us the mystery of his will, according to his good pleasure which he hath purposed in himself:

Think about this. Before God created, there was only Him in His perfection. At that time, God purposed or determined in advance what He is doing today in the Dispensation of Grace. We continue in Ephesians. Verses 10–11:

10 That in the dispensation of the fulness of times he might gather together in one all things in Christ, both which are in heaven, and which are on earth; even in him: 11 In whom also we have obtained an inheritance, being predestinated according to the purpose of him who worketh all things after the counsel of his own will:

Everything that happens is according to God's will.

He purposed in advance that His Son will die on the Cross. He determined the how, when, and the why.

Consider our last reference. Titus 1:1–2:

> 1 **Paul, a servant of God, and an apostle of Jesus Christ, according to the faith of God's elect, and the acknowledging of the truth which is after godliness; 2 In hope of eternal life, which God, that cannot lie, promised before the world began;**

In other words, God the Father, God the Son, and God the Holy Spirit counseled together before the world began. They agreed to all this and, furthermore, to keep it a mystery until Christ Himself revealed it to Paul who is the Apostle to the Gentiles. Verse 3:

> 3 **But hath in due times manifested his word through preaching, which is committed unto me according to the commandment of God our Saviour;**

At the perfect time, predetermined eons in advance, Christ made known the "mystery" to the Apostle Paul. He was chosen to carry this message to the Gentiles.

We return to our text. Romans 5:6:

**6 For when we were yet without strength, in due time Christ died for the ungodly.**

An important fact to consider here is that, according to God, everybody is ungodly. As humans, we compare ourselves with other people and say, "Hey, I'm a pretty good person. I'm better than most." However, God's standard is perfection and, by His standard, everyone is ungodly. Every single man, woman, and child born is a direct descendant of Adam who fell and, therefore, is ungodly. Yet Christ died for the ungodly!

We move on. Verse 7:

**7 For scarcely for a righteous man will one die: yet peradventure for a good man some would even dare to die.**

Paul says *scarcely* means *hardly* or *rarely*. There would be rarely or hardly a chance that someone would be willing to die for a righteous man. What about dying for an ungodly sinner? Certainly, there would be no chance anyone would be willing to die for the ungodly, right? We are not ungodly, are we? Some people get the idea that God got a deal when He saved them. God does not look at people and say, "I think I'll die for them because they're pretty good folks." No, God did not look at us and say, "I think these people deserve it. I will  shed My blood for them." No. All of us are ungodly. Verse 8:

**8 But God commendeth his love toward us, in that, while we were yet sinners, Christ died for us.**

The very reason Christ died for us is because we were sinners and unable to save ourselves. He loved us that much to take our sin upon Himself and die for us, the ungodly. He became sin for us. He took our punishment and died on the Cross. Being dead, He was buried in our place. However, the grave could not hold a righteous Man, so God raised Him from the dead with power. Today, Christ imputes His righteousness to all who believe. We are offered the gift of right-standing because of what God did for us through Christ His Son. Friends,, that is true *Love*. That is *Amazing Grace!*

There is something I would like you to see in the Gospel of John. Jesus is speaking with His disciples. John 15:13:

**13 Greater love hath no man than this, that a man lay down his life for his**

**friends.**

Jesus talks about a man laying down his life for his friends. However, the next verse gives us an insight into its meaning. Verse 14:

> 14 **Ye are my friends, if ye do whatsoever I command you.**

Jesus is specifying who His friends are and how He knows that they are His friends. His friends are those that keep His commandments. The word *commandments* is another word for *Law*. As Gentiles, we were aliens and strangers from the covenants. The Gentiles who did not follow the Law and commandments, as taught in the four Gospels, would mean they were His enemies!

Now, let us move on. Romans 5:9–11:

> 9 **Much more then, being now justified by his blood, we shall be saved from wrath through him.** 10 **For if, <u>when we were enemies</u>, <u>we were reconciled to God by the death of his Son</u>, much more, being reconciled, we shall be saved by his life.** 11 **And not only so, but we also joy in God through our Lord Jesus Christ, by whom we have now re-**

**ceived the atonement.**

Christ willingly laid down His life for His enemies. In the Age of Law, Christ talked about laying down His life "for His friends," those who kept His commandments. However, in this current age, the Dispensation of Grace, we find that Jesus laid down His life "for His enemies."

Above, Paul wrote "being now justified by His blood." Are we justified through faith or justified by His blood? The answer is: both! Romans 3:21–26:

> **21 But now the righteousness of God without the law is manifested, being witnessed by the law and the prophets; 22 Even the righteousness of God which is by faith of Jesus Christ unto all and upon all them that believe: for there is no difference: 23 For all have sinned, and come short of the glory of God; 24 Being justified freely by his grace through the redemption that is in Christ Jesus: 25 Whom God hath set forth to be a propitiation through faith in his blood, to declare his righteousness for the remission of sins that are past, through the forbearance of God;**

**26** <u>To declare, I say, at this time his right-eousness: that he might be just, and the justifier of him which believeth in Je-sus.</u>

Our redemption is "through faith in His blood" and all that Christ did to accomplish that. He Who was free from sin shed His own blood to pay for our sins. It is Christ's righteousness that He gives to those who believe what He did on their behalf.

In the 1970s, there was a well-known preacher on the radio who said that the blood of Christ was not the issue. I am sure he regrets saying those words now. Later, he tried to recant it. Remember this fact. The blood of Christ is critical to our salvation. Revelation 1:5:

> **5 And from Jesus Christ, who is the faithful witness, and the first begotten of the dead, and the prince of the kings of the earth. Unto him that loved us, and** <u>**washed us from our sins in his own blood,**</u>

Here is another reference to Christ's blood. Acts 20:28:

**28 Take heed therefore unto yourselves,**

**and to all the flock, over the which the Holy Ghost hath made you overseers, to feed the church of God, <u>which he hath purchased with his own blood</u>.**

Anyone who says that "the blood" is not important is wrong.

Paul wrote, "being now justified by his blood, we shall be saved from wrath through him" (Rom. 5:9). In the Gospel of Matthew, John the Baptist is making converts by preaching that the Kingdom was at hand. He realizes that some of the religious leaders were there listening to him. Matthew 3:7:

**7 But when he saw many of the Pharisees and Sadducees come to his baptism, he said unto them, O generation of vipers, who hath warned you to flee from the wrath to come?**

The phrase the "wrath to come" is a direct reference to the Tribulation. The Jews know it as Jacob's time of trouble. (See Jeremiah 30:7.) It will be seven years of testing for the Jews. Paul teaches those saved by grace that they have already been justified. They have been declared righteous in His Son and saved from the "wrath to come."

Paul writes these words of assurance to Grace Believers. 1 Thessalonians 1:9–10:

**9 For they themselves shew of us what manner of entering in we had unto you, and how ye turned to God from idols to serve the living and true God; 10 And to wait for his Son from heaven, whom he raised from the dead, even Jesus, <u>which [who] delivered us from the wrath to come.</u>**

Consider this to be an historical fact: the Rapture will occur prior to the beginning of the Tribulation. Those saved by grace through faith, called the Body of Christ, will be *caught up* to be with Christ at His Appearing. This is not to be confused with His Second Coming to the Jews. It is His Appearing or *His Calling* for which Grace Believers wait. The Rapture is *pre-tribulational*. The Lord will appear and we will be delivered from the wrath to come.

One might ask, "Then who will experience the wrath of God?" It must be those under the Law since with the Law comes judgment and condemnation. If someone puts themselves under the Law, guess what they have for their future? Under the Law, they are going to be judged and will experience the wrath of God. Today, there is no judgment during the Age of

142

Grace. Presently, no one's sins are being punished, but the time of judgment is coming.

There are two kinds of wrath. There are two kinds of judgments. There is the judgment of the unbeliever in Hell and there is the wrath of God to be poured out on the earth during the Tribulation. Some people will not only go through the wrath of God on earth, but they will also experience His eternal judgment in a place called Hell. Therefore, we want as many as possible to be saved by grace!

Paul writes a lot about *reconciliation* and *being reconciled*. 2 Corinthians 5:18–21:

> 18 **And all things are of God, who hath reconciled us to himself by Jesus Christ, and hath given to us the ministry of reconciliation; 19 To wit, that God was in Christ, reconciling the world unto himself, not imputing their trespasses unto them; and hath committed unto us the word of reconciliation. 20 Now then we are ambassadors for Christ, as though God did beseech you by us: we pray you in Christ's stead, be ye reconciled to God. 21 For he hath made him to be sin for us, who knew no sin; that we might be made the righteousness of God in**

**him.**

When we read, "God was in Christ reconciling the world unto Himself," do not make the mistake of thinking this is universal salvation for everyone. Christ provides the means by which reconciliation for the world *is possible.* However, He does not force His free gift of salvation on anyone. This would violate their *free will.* He provides reconciliation through the Cross, but `He does not make anyone accept His gracious offer. Individuals must choose to believe the gospel in order to be saved. That is why Paul pleads for people to "be ye reconciled to God." Since we all have *free will,* it is our own choice to make. Paul writes emphatically "as though God did beseech you by us: we pray you in Christ's stead, be ye reconciled to God." It will be the Grace Believers who take upon themselves the ministry of reconciliation who ask others to be "reconciled to God."

I would like us to look at a verse again. This time, we will pay particular attention to the different verb tenses. Romans 5:9:

> 9 **Much more then, <u>being now justified</u> by his blood, <u>we shall be saved</u> from wrath through him.**

Presently, "being now justified" by His blood we

continue in our current state of justification. As Grace Believers, we were justified and declared righteous. That was behind us. Notice that the next verb changes to a future tense. It declares that we "shall be saved" from the wrath to come. That wrath is the Tribulation.

We are going to look at several verses to shed light on this. Romans 4:22–25:

> 22 **And therefore it was imputed to him for righteousness. 23 Now it was not written for his sake alone, that it was imputed to him; 24 But for us also, to whom it shall be imputed, if we believe on him that raised up Jesus our Lord from the dead; 25 Who was delivered for our offences, and was raised again for our justification.**

Because of what Christ accomplished through His work on the Cross, God declared Him to be righteous by raising Him from the dead. His righteousness is then imputed or transferred to all who believe in His death, burial, and resurrection. His death paid for our offences and He was raised from the dead for our justification. In other words, His life is in us. Our new life is in Christ!

Now, look at Romans 6:3–5:

**3 Know ye not, that so many of us as were baptized into Jesus Christ were baptized into his death? 4 Therefore we are <u>buried with him</u> by baptism into death: that like as Christ was raised up from the dead by the glory of the Father, even so we also should walk in newness of life. 5 For <u>if we have been planted together in the likeness of his death, we shall be also in the likeness of his resurrection:</u>**

Here, Paul talks about the Spirit baptizing us into the Body of Christ. This has nothing to do with water baptism which is part of the Kingdom Gospel. We were buried with Him spiritually by our baptism into His death. Then, being *in Christ*, we were raised with Him from the dead by the Father. At the Rapture, we will receive our glorified bodies like Christ's.

Let us read Colossians 1:26–27:

**26 Even the mystery which hath been hid from ages and from generations, but now is made manifest to his saints: 27 To whom God would make known what is**

the riches of <u>the glory of this mystery</u> among the Gentiles; which is <u>Christ in you, the hope of glory</u>:

In the previous chapter, we learned that the phrase "the hope of glory" refers to the Rapture. We have the eternal life of Christ in us. When we are raptured, we will be with Him forever. That, my friends, is our *hope of glory*.

Now, turn back to Romans 5:11:

11 **And not only so, but we also joy in God through our Lord Jesus Christ, by whom we have now received the atonement.**

Grace Believers received "the atonement." The word *atonement* means *the act of making compensation for wrong-doing*. It reconciles two parties who are at odds. The word *atonement* is used frequently in the Old Testament. The Levitical priests would go daily into the Temple or Tabernacle to offer sacrifices *atoning* for the sins of Israel. In Romans 5, Paul is dealing with something similar, but there is a difference. We need to see the distinction between how the word *atonement* is used in the Old Testament and how it is used here. There is a dispensational difference. Let us look at Hebrews which was written to the Jews.

Hebrews 10:1–4:

> 1 For the law having a shadow of good things to come, and not the very image of the things, can never with those sacrifices which they offered year by year continually make the comers thereunto perfect. 2 For then would they not have ceased to be offered? because that the worshippers once purged should have had no more conscience of sins. 3 But in those sacrifices there is a remembrance again made of sins every year. 4 For it is not possible that the blood of bulls and of goats should take away sins.

Notice it says that their sacrifices could never make them perfect. Otherwise, why would they need to continue them year after year? These sacrifices of blood from animals could not take away their sins. It could only cover them. Therefore, these sacrifices the priests offered were only an *atonement* for their sin. They had to keep doing that over and over again. They were a *type* which means a *foreshadowing* of the Messiah's atonement which would be permanent. The former atonements only covered their sins temporarily and kept their sins in remission.

When we read Peter's speech at Pentecost, it

provides additional support for this. Acts 2:37-38:

> 37 **Now when they heard this, they were pricked in their heart, and said unto Peter and to the rest of the apostles, Men and brethren, what shall we do?** 38 **Then Peter said unto them, Repent, and be baptized every one of you in the name of Jesus Christ <u>for the remission of sins</u>, and ye shall receive the gift of the Holy Ghost.**

The death of Christ on the Cross was the one final atonement of which those previous sacrifices were only a *type*. However, for Grace Believers, we do not need someone going into a tabernacle day after day making continual sacrifices for our sin. We have the one final atonement through the blood of Christ shed for us on the Cross.

Understanding *atonement* is easy once we realize that it is a dispensational issue. For Grace Believers, Christ is our complete and final *atonement*. We are made perfect *in Him*. On the other hand, Hebrews talks about sacrifices being continually made for Israel to atone for their sins. Those saved under the Gospel of the Kingdom have a High Priest Who intercedes for them daily. Hebrews 7:23–25:

**23** And they truly were many priests, because they were not suffered [allowed]
to continue by reason of death: **24** But
this man [Christ], because he contin-
ueth ever, hath an unchangeable priesthood. **25** Wherefore he is able also to
save them to the uttermost that come
unto God by him, seeing he ever liveth
to make intercession for them.

Israel's priests who served in the earthly Temple or Tabernacle could not continue because they
died. However, their Messiah is presently in the
heavenly Tabernacle and continually serves to make
intercession for them. This High Priest will live forever. Daily atonements will continue for Israel until
the Messiah forgives their sins. This will occur at the
conclusion of the Tribulation when their Messiah returns to earth at His Second Coming. This must not
be confused with His Appearing in the sky at the
Rapture.

The distinction between the Gospel of the
Kingdom and the Gospel of the Grace makes complete sense once understood. Here is a perfect summary of what we have discussed so far. Colossians
2:10–15:

**10** And ye are complete in him, which is

the head of all principality and power: 11 In whom also ye are circumcised with the circumcision made without hands, in putting off the body of the sins of the flesh by the circumcision of Christ:

12 Buried with him in baptism, wherein also ye are risen with him through the faith of the operation of God, who hath raised him from the dead. 13 And you, being dead in your sins and the uncircumcision of your flesh, hath he quickened together with him, having forgiven you all trespasses;

14 Blotting out the handwriting of ordinances that was against us, which was contrary to us, and took it out of the way, nailing it to his cross; 15 And having spoiled principalities and powers, he made a shew of them openly, triumphing over them in it.

We will complete Romans 5 in the next chapter.

# 9

# Romans 5 (Part III)

We will look at a block of text and then break it down verse by verse. Romans 5:12–17:

12 Wherefore, as by one man sin entered into the world, and death by sin; and so death passed upon all men, for that all have sinned: 13 (For until the law sin was in the world: but sin is not imputed when there is no law.

14 Nevertheless death reigned from Adam to Moses, even over them that had not sinned after the similitude of Adam's transgression, who is the figure of him that was to come. 15 But not as the offence, so also is the free gift. For if through the offence of one many be dead, much more the grace of God, and the gift by grace, which is by one man,

Jesus Christ, hath abounded unto many.

16 And not as it was by one that sinned, so is the gift: for the judgment was by one to condemnation, but the free gift is of many offences unto justification. 17 For if by one man's offence death reigned by one; much more they which receive abundance of grace and of the gift of righteousness shall reign in life by one, Jesus Christ.)

We can clearly see in the above passage that death came as the result of sin. Even before the Law was given to Moses, all mankind had inherited Adam's sin nature. For that reason, all must die.

James wrote about this later in his epistle to the Kingdom Believers. James 1:14–15:

14 But every man is tempted, when he is drawn away of his own lust, and enticed. 15 Then when lust hath conceived, it bringeth forth sin: and sin, when it is finished, bringeth forth death.

This explains why Adam died and all those after him must die. Each of us has Adam's sin nature from what is called *original sin.* We find this in Romans 5:12:

> 12 **Wherefore, as by one man sin entered into the world, and death by sin; and so death passed upon all men, for that all have sinned:**

What does the first part of that verse tell us? There was no death until there was sin. So as the result of Adam's sin, death passed upon all men. All have sinned in Adam and, for this reason, all must die.

We continue. Verse 13:

> 13 **(For until the law sin was in the world: but sin is not imputed when there is no law.**

This is simple. If God had not yet given the Law, then the Law would not have existed and, therefore, it could not condemn. That does not mean that man did not sin before the Law. Rather, it means the there was no Law present to condemn us. Adam was not given the Law, yet he died. Why? Because he disobeyed the one instruction God gave him. Genesis 2:16–17:

> 16 **And the LORD God commanded the**

man, saying, Of every tree of the garden thou mayest freely eat: 17 But of the tree of the knowledge of good and evil, thou shalt not eat of it: for in the day that thou eatest thereof thou shalt surely die.

Paul makes a comparison between Adam and Christ saying both of them were a first. Romans 5:14:

14 **Nevertheless death reigned from Adam to Moses, even over them that had not sinned after the similitude of Adam's transgression, who is the figure of him that was to come.**

Death came from Adam's original sin and continues to apply to all. The wages of sin is death. (See Romans 6:23.) Paul makes a point here. Even though there was no Mosaic Law at the time of Adam, when he disobeyed God, he suffered the consequence of his action. Doing so, he caused all to die. Sin is still sin. The consequence of disobeying God is death. This applied even before the Law.

Adam was a figure, a representation, or image of Someone Who was yet to come. Verses 15–16:

15 **But not as the offence, so also is the free gift. For if through the offence of**

one many be dead, much more the grace of God, and the gift by grace, which is by one man, Jesus Christ, hath abounded unto many. 16 And not as it was by one that sinned, so is the gift: for the judgment was by one to condemnation, but the free gift is of many offences unto justification.

We see that through the offence of one, referring to Adam, many are dead. Paul shows that, unlike Adam's sin, one man, our Lord Jesus Christ, brings the offer of the *free gift* of grace. Again, through the offence of one, Adam, many people die. How many? Everyone in the human race. The word *many* in this context means *all*. However, by the grace of God through the act of one Man, Jesus Christ, grace may abound to many. Here, the reason why *many* cannot be interpreted as *all* is that not everybody will choose to believe the Gospel of Grace.

Concerning this issue of "many" and "all" being used, let us look in 1 Corinthians. These verses also contrast Adam with Christ. 1 Corinthians 15 21–22:

21 For since by man came death, by man came also the resurrection of the dead. 22 For as in Adam all die, even so in

## Christ shall all be made alive.

In verse 22, Paul used the word *all* in both places. Interesting. It is true that in Christ shall *all* be made alive. This makes the resurrection of *all* possible. Christ told His disciples, "Marvel not at this: for the hour is coming, in the which all that are in the graves shall hear his voice, And shall come forth; they that have done good, unto the resurrection of life; and they that have done evil, unto the resurrection of damnation" (Jn. 5:28-29). Those who trust in the finished work of Christ upon the Cross will enter into the joy of fellowship with their Lord and Savior.

We continue. Romans 5:17–18:

> 17 **For if by one man's offence death reigned by one; much more they which receive abundance of grace and of the gift of righteousness shall reign in life by one, Jesus Christ.) 18 Therefore as by the offence of one judgment came upon all men to condemnation; even so by the righteousness of one the free gift came upon all men unto justification of life.**

Paul compares the condemnation brought upon all through Adam's sin to the righteousness available freely through Jesus Christ. It is a free gift. We had no choice under Adam's condemnation, but now we have a choice to receive Christ's righteousness. His righteousness covers all the offenses and gives righteousness to all who believe in His work done on their behalf. By Adam, death reigned. However, with the gift of grace, righteousness reigns in Christ.

To make a point, let us go back and look at verses 15–18 one more time. We need to count the number of times we see Paul use the following words: *free, gift,* and *grace.* If my eyes are working right, then I see *free* used three times, *gift* used six times, and *grace* used three times in just these four verses. Paul is really emphasizing the fact that salvation by *grace* is a *gift.* It is absolutely *free!*

There is something I would like to share with you. The following is a good example to illustrate the contrast between Adam and Christ. 1 Corinthians 15:44–49:

> **44 It is sown a natural body; it is raised a spiritual body. There is a natural body, and there is a spiritual body. 45 And so it is written, The first man Adam was made a living soul; the last Adam was made a quickening spirit. 46 Howbeit that was not first which is spiritual, but that which is natural; and afterward that**

which is spiritual.

**47 The first man is of the earth, earthy: the second man is the Lord from heaven. 48 As is the earthy, such are they also that are earthy: and as is the heavenly, such are they also that are heavenly. 49 And as we have borne the image of the earthy, we shall also bear the image of the heavenly.**

Adam was given life. However, Christ, Who is the second and last Adam, is the Giver of life Himself. The first Man, Adam, is of the earth, a creature created by God's hands, and given the breath of life. The second Man, Christ Who is the Lord from heaven, is heavenly and the Creator of all things.

Here is another comparison. 1 Corinthians 15:22–23:

**22 For as in Adam all die, even so in Christ shall all be made alive. 23 But every man in his own order: Christ the firstfruits; afterward they that are Christ's at his coming.**

Notice the order of the resurrection. Christ was the firstfruits because He was resurrected first; then, those who are in Christ at His Appearing will follow. That would be the Rapture.

Let us return to our text. Romans 5:19:

19 **For as by one man's disobedience many were made sinners, so by the obedience of one shall many be made righteous.**

When Paul says, "the free gift came upon all men unto justification of life" (v. 18), he does not mean that all men are automatically saved. We must choose to believe the gospel in order for it to apply to us. We have to use our free will and choose to believe it. Then, at that point of believing, we receive the free gift. However, we can also freely choose to reject the free gift. Some people will spend eternity paying for their sins because they rejected the free gift offered to us all.

Therefore, from the sin of one man, judgment came upon all men leading to condemnation. In a similar manner, the righteousness of one Man, the free gift of salvation came to be offered to all men through justification. Because of Adam's original sin, all men were made sinners because we all inherited Adam's sin nature. Contrary to this, by the faithfulness or obedience of Christ, many shall be made righteous. In Adam, we have judgment. In Christ, we have righteousness!

Let us continue. Verse 20:

**20 Moreover the law entered, that the offence might abound. But where sin abounded, grace did much more abound:**

What does Paul mean when he writes "the Law entered, that the offence might abound?" Well, the giving of the Law to Moses increased sin because the Law goes into great detail about all the different sins that man can commit. The Law is like a mirror. It shows us all our imperfections – every single sin we have committed. In that way, the Law makes the number of offenses increase by showing us our own sins; not just those of Adam. Some Christians believe that they can keep all the rules in order to get them into Heaven. They are basically delusional. It shows a clear ignorance of what the Scriptures actually teach. Out of pride, man wants to think that he is able to merit God's salvation through his own righteousness.

We finish this chapter with verse 21:

**21 That as sin hath reigned unto death,**

**even so might grace reign through righteousness unto eternal life by Jesus Christ our Lord.**

Even with the addition of the Law which exposed man to hundreds and hundreds of different possible sins, the quantity of sins will never exceed the sufficiency of God's grace. His grace exceeds whatever offense of the Law we have committed or will commit. We see the words "as sin hath reigned unto death." We know what the verb *to reign* means. It is like a evil king on his throne ruling over his kingdom. It means having dominion over everything. Sin continued to reign over our lives, having dominion over us until death. However, His grace reigns over us through righteousness leading not to death but unto eternal life through Jesus Christ our Lord! What reigns today in this Dispensation of Grace? According to this last verse, grace reigns through righteousness unto eternal life. That is why we call it the Dispensation of Grace. God is dispensing His grace to everyone. The questions is: will they accept His offer of grace?

In closing, there is a hymn entitled "Grace Greater Than All Our Sin." It was written in 1910 by Julia H. Johnston. It was verses of Scripture like these that stirred her heart to pen these words:

Marvelous grace of our loving Lord,
Grace that exceeds our sin and our guilt!
Marvelous, infinite, matchless grace,
Freely bestowed on all who believe!

# 10

## Romans 6 (Part I)

Paul continues to build upon the preceding chapters. Romans 6:1–2:

> 1 **What shall we say then? Shall we continue in sin, that grace may abound? 2 God forbid. How shall we, that are dead to sin, live any longer therein?**

Why does Paul begin with this question? What have we learned? Having the information presented so far freshly in our minds, he leads us to this question, "Shall we continue in sin, that grace may abound?" It may surprise you that this is a common question asked by those who hear about God's grace for the first time. Paul responds, "God forbid!" That is a very strong "Certainly not!" He continues, "How shall we that are dead to sin live in sin any longer?" Paul will address Grace Believers for the remainder of this chapter.

How do we deal with *sin* which is also called the old nature or the Adamic nature? Specifically, how do we deal with this as a member of the Body of Christ? We cannot deal with our old sin nature by the Law. We learned that it does not work. For the only thing that the Law can do is expose sin and show us that we need a Savior. The Law does nothing for us with regard to our salvation or our walk with the Lord. Why? Because its sole purpose is to show us that we are sinners and condemn us. The Law does not give life. Paul continues his introduction by asking us, "How can we, who are dead in sin, live in sin any longer?"

He gives us the answer and introduces us to what I call *positional truth*. The *position* which God put us in as a result of believing the gospel is "in" His Son, our Lord Jesus Christ. Therefore, our new identity is *in Christ*. We are a new creature *in Christ*. We have been given, as a new creature, a new identity *in Christ* and, with that, a new purpose. This is something new which we have never had before. In fact, neither Gentile nor Jew has ever had this opportunity before. Our *position* of being *in Christ* is something completely new! But wait, there is more.

As a result of this new position of being *in Christ*, there are some new spiritual blessings that come with being members of the Body of Christ. Do you remember Paul asking, "How can we who are dead to sin, live in sin any longer?" His first point regarding our *new position* is that we are dead to sin. Paul is not talking about the sins we commit daily. He is talking about our position *in Christ*. We are dead to sin as far as God is concerned. Stay with me here and follow closely. So, what is going on here? Paul explains that if we are dead to sin, then why would we continue to live in sin any longer? We see that God wants us to walk by faith in that *positional truth*. He has already declared us *dead to sin*, and he wants us to walk by faith knowing the truth that, again, we are dead to sin!

This has to do with renewing our minds. It is about looking at ourselves the same way God sees us, not the way each of us sees ourselves. Verse 3:

> 3 **Know ye not, that so many of us as were baptized into Jesus Christ were baptized into his death?**

Paul uses the phrase "know ye not" about ten times in his letters to those saved by grace through faith. It always has to do with who we are in Christ. He is reminding us about something we should already know, and if we do not, then it is something we ought to know going forward. The concept of being baptized into Jesus Christ also means we were baptized into His death. Why is this idea so foreign? It is because, even though it is true, it is not taught in most churches. Most churches teach that once someone has "given their life to Christ," they need to do good deeds, and if they sin, they must ask Jesus to forgive them. That is exactly the opposite to what Paul is telling us here.

What does it mean to be "baptized into Christ?" In Scripture, the word *baptism* does not always refer to water. In the Gospel of Matthew, John the Baptist is speaking to the Pharisees who are the religious leaders of Israel. Matthew 3:11:

> 11 **I indeed baptize you with water unto repentance: but he that cometh after me is mightier than I, whose shoes I am not worthy to bear: he shall baptize you with the Holy Ghost, and with fire:**

What does he mean? First of all, I see three baptisms here. There is the baptism with water, which is what John the Baptist was doing. Then, there is the reference to the Lord Jesus Christ baptizing with the Holy Ghost. Later in the judgment, there will be a baptism with fire. Again, John tells us that Christ is going to baptize some people with the Holy Ghost and some with fire.

Let us continue by reading the remainder of this passage. Verse 12:

> 12 **Whose fan is in his hand, and he will throughly purge his floor, and gather his wheat into the garner; but he will burn up the chaff with unquenchable fire.**

John is writing to Kingdom Believers. The wheat of His harvest are those people who believe the Kingdom Gospel and are baptized. However, those who reject Him are not baptized by the Holy Spirit. They will be burned up with unquenchable fire. Many Bible students will recognize the words "unquenchable fire" as referring to Hell and eternal separation from God.

So far, we see three baptisms: one with water, one with the Holy Ghost, and one with fire. We do not want the last one. That baptism is judgment by unquenchable fire. We do not need the first one which is water baptism. It is part of the Kingdom Gospel which requires repentance and water baptism. In Acts 2, after hearing Peter's accusations concerning Israel killing their Messiah, Peter was asked by the Jews at Pentecost, "Men and brethren, what shall we do?" Look at how Peter responds. He tells them to "repent, and be baptized every one of you in the name of Jesus Christ for the remission of sins" (vv. 37–38). This has absolutely nothing to do with our being baptized *into Christ*.

Let us go to 1 Corinthians 12:12–13:

**12 For as the body is one, and hath many members, and all the members of that one body, being many, are one body: so also is Christ. 13 For by one Spirit are we all baptized into one body, whether we be Jews or Gentiles, whether we be bond or free; and have been all made to drink into one Spirit.**

The Body of Christ has many members and all these members are one Body. It is by one Spirit that we all are baptized into that one Body. That body is the Body of Christ! Whether we are Jews or Gentiles, whether we are bond or free, we are all made to drink into one Spirit.

In Matthew 3, John the Baptist says that he baptized with water. However, referring to the Christ, we are told that Jesus would be the Baptizer and He is going to baptize some with the Holy Spirit. What we find in 1 Corinthians 12 is something entirely different. There we find that the Holy Spirit is doing the baptizing. In Matthew, they were baptized into the Kingdom. However, for those saved by grace, it is the Spirit Who baptizes us into the Body of Christ. This happens the moment that we believe the Gospel of Grace. Then, the Holy Spirit seals us until His Calling. Friends, this would be a good place to use the word: *Hallelujah!*

Let us move on. Romans 6:3:

**3 Know ye not, that so many of us as were baptized into Jesus Christ were baptized into his death?**

This is a *positional truth*. When the Holy Spirit baptized us *into Christ,* we were baptized into His death. So, *positionally*, we died *in Christ* when He died on the Cross. We were baptized into His death. Most importantly, we were justified *in Christ* when God raised Him from the dead. The significance of this was not understood until it was given to the Apostle Paul. For this reason, it is referred to as "the revelation of the mystery."

When we believe the Gospel for the first time, at that moment, we are spiritually baptized "into His death." We "spiritually" participate in His death, His burial, and His resurrection. Verse 4:

**4 Therefore we are buried with him by baptism into death: that like as Christ was raised up from the dead by the glory of the Father, even so we also should walk in newness of life.**

To understand the significance of this, let us see it the way God sees it. When Christ died on the cross, we died too. When He was buried in the tomb, we were buried too. When He rose from the dead the third day, spiritually, we rose also. That is the simplest way to explain this *positional truth*. Therefore, being raised from the dead, we should walk in newness of life. This *positional truth* is how we need to see ourselves. God now sees Christ when He looks at us: dead, buried, and risen again. All of this was done for one purpose: that we can walk in newness of life. Knowing this, we must walk by faith!

Dear saints, that is how we change the way we behave. This is how we correct bad behavior in our walk with the Lord. We recognize that we are dead, buried, and resurrected with Christ. If we are raised to walk in newness of life, then we should behave like we have a new life. This is something completely different from what most church denominations teach. Therefore, do not read into this whatever you have been previously taught. This is different! We need to develop this line of thinking further.

What does it mean to plant something? We go to the store, buy some seeds, come home, and go into our backyard. Then, we dig some holes and plant the seeds. Why? It is because we want the seeds to grow, right? This is what Paul is talking about in verse 5:

> 5 **For if we have been planted together in the likeness of his death, we shall be also in the likeness of his resurrection:**

When Paul writes that, "we have been planted together in the likeness of his death," he is talking about His burial. There is an interesting story in the Gospel of John where some Gentiles, called Greeks, came to see Jesus, but He would not see them. Instead, He gives a prophetic response about a seed needing to die before it comes to life. John 12:20–24:

> 20 **And there were certain Greeks among them that came up to worship at the feast: 21 The same came therefore to Philip, which was of Bethsaida of Galilee, and desired him, saying, Sir, we would see Jesus. 22 Philip cometh and telleth Andrew: and again Andrew and Philip tell Jesus. 23 And Jesus answered**

**them, saying, The hour is come, that the Son of man should be glorified. 24 Verily, verily, I say unto you, Except a corn of wheat fall into the ground and die, it abideth alone: but if it die, it bringeth forth much fruit.**

A seed itself is not alive. It is dead. However, when it is buried in the ground, it comes to new life and, in doing so, produces more seeds. Even nature teaches us about death, burial, and resurrection. How interesting is that!

Paul continues. Romans 6:6–7:

**6 Knowing this, that our old man is crucified with him, that the body of sin might be destroyed, that henceforth we should not serve sin. 7 For he that is dead is freed from sin.**

Our old man, our Adamic nature, was crucified with Christ. The reason for this was that the body of sin must die in order that we would no longer be a slave to sin. Therefore, now that we are *dead* to sin, then we are *free* from sin.

I like to use the following illustration: We go to a funeral. There is a corpse laid out in the coffin surrounded by beautiful flowers. Several of his old drinking buddies approach the corpse individually and make various suggestions of sinful things he could do. Can the corpse get up and go sin? No, he cannot. He is dead and dead people can no longer sin! This is how God wants us to see ourselves. He wants us to see ourselves as dead to our old man and alive in Christ. This is how we deal with our sin nature. Yes, it is a daily battle. It is a continuous struggle. However, it becomes much easier once we understand the importance of what these verses are teaching us. This is a very powerful and important chapter in Romans. I hope you agree that rushing through it would be doing the Word of God and the reader a disservice.

I would like to stop here and ask you to think about the foundational truths we have just discussed. Think about your own *position in Christ* and your inability to sin because you have died, were buried, and you have risen again *in Christ*. Think about that *positional truth*. We will continue with the remainder of Romans 6 in the next chapter.

# 11

Romans 6 (Part II)

We learned about our new position in Christ. It is important for us to see ourselves as God sees us. Yes, our new spiritual *position* is in Christ, but we remain in our physical bodies. That is our physical *position.* Our daily walk is something that I call *practice.* In Romans 6, Paul deals with the *position* and *practice* of Grace Believers. As we continue, we will look at these two dynamics in greater depth. Spiritually, we have our *position* or standing in Christ. As we wait for the Rapture, we have our current *practice* in the flesh.

Let us go back to the original question Paul wrote at the beginning of the chapter, "Shall we continue in sin, that grace may abound?" (Rom. 6:1). Paul answered, "God forbid!" and has gone into great detail throughout this chapter. He explains why those saved by grace through faith should not continue in sin. We have faith in what Christ has done. In Him, we were baptized into His death, burial, and resurrection. Let us consider the word *baptism*. Colossians 2:11–13:

> **11 In whom also ye are circumcised with the circumcision made without hands, in putting off the body of the sins of the flesh by the circumcision of Christ: 12 Buried with him in baptism, wherein also ye are risen with him through the faith of the operation of God, who hath raised him from the dead. 13 And you, being dead in your sins and the uncircumcision of your flesh, hath he quickened together with him, having forgiven you all trespasses;**

We have a circumcision made without hands. Circumcision is a surgical procedure. However, Paul is speaking about a *spiritual* circumcision just like the *spiritual* baptism in verse 12. He explains that we were *spiritually* buried with Christ in our baptism. Also, we are *spiritually* risen with Him. How is this possible? It is through faith in God Who raised Christ from the dead. This operation of God is sometimes referred to as *the power of God*. Our baptism is spiritual and has nothing to do with the ritual of being immersed in water. It is about having faith in something that God has already done for us. It takes place the moment we believe the gospel.

Many teach that water baptism is an ordinance of the Church. The word *ordinance* means a *law, rule, precept,* or *statute.* Colossians 2:14:

> **14 Blotting out the handwriting of ordinances that was against us, which was contrary to us, and took it out of the way, nailing it to his cross;**

On the Cross, Christ forgave all sins completely. God made having faith in Him the only requirement. He blotted out all requirements and that includes all ordinances. Therefore, at the moment we accept the gospel as truth, we are buried with Christ into His death, a *positional truth.* Furthermore, in Christ we are raised from the dead by the glory of the Father so that we can walk in Christ with our new spiritual life, both in *position* and in *practice.* Bear with me a moment as this concerns our *position* and *practice.* Paul compares it to planting a seed by making an association with our spiritual baptism and His burial. Colossians 2:6–11:

> **6 As ye have therefore received Christ Jesus the Lord, so walk ye in him: 7 Rooted and built up in him, and stab-**

lished in the faith, as ye have been taught, abounding therein with thanksgiving. 8 Beware lest any man spoil you through philosophy and vain deceit, after the tradition of men, after the rudiments of the world, and not after Christ.

9 For in him dwelleth all the fulness of the Godhead bodily. 10 And ye are complete in him, which is the head of all principality and power: 11 In whom also ye are circumcised with the circumcision made without hands, in putting off the body of the sins of the flesh by the circumcision of Christ:

Can you see the concept clearly now? We have our *position* in Christ and then there is our *practice*. By faith, we walk in the *position* that He has placed us in.

Now, look at Colossians 3:8–9:

8 But now ye also put off all these; anger, wrath, malice, blasphemy, filthy communication out of your mouth. 9 Lie not one to another, seeing that ye have put off the old man with his deeds;

Paul is saying this is a *positional truth*. We have put off the old man because he is dead. Therefore, if God has put off the old man for us, what should we do? We should put off the old man by putting off his deeds. Verse 10:

> **10 And have put on the new man, which is renewed in knowledge after the image of him that created him:**

The *new man* was created after Jesus Christ. We did not create him. We did not become a new creature on our own. We became a new creature as a result of Christ Who made us into a new creature. We put on this new man, this new creature, by faith. It is a faith choice we make. Yes, he saved us. Yes, He gave us eternal salvation, but there is more, my friend. God has made us who and what we are now. He has placed us *in Christ,* and now, we must choose, by faith, to walk *in that truth.* We need to say to ourselves, "If I am dead to sin, then I am going to live like I am dead to sin!" Daily we need to recognize that, *by faith,* we are a new creature in Christ. Therefore, we should choose, *by faith,* to act like a new creature in Christ.

Let us look at Ephesians 4:23–24:

> **23 And be renewed in the spirit of your**

mind; 24 And that ye put on the new
man, which after God is created in
righteousness and true holiness.

It may make more sense if we interpret it as being
"renewed by the Spirit in our mind." There is another reference for us to consider. Romans 12:1–2:

1 I beseech you therefore, brethren, by
the mercies of God, that ye present your
bodies a living sacrifice, holy, acceptable unto God, which is your reasonable
service. 2 And be not conformed to this
world: but be ye transformed by the renewing of your mind, that ye may prove
what is that good, and acceptable, and
perfect, will of God.

Paul makes the same point above by saying we
should be "transformed by the renewing of your
mind." How do we renew our mind? We do it by getting into the Word of God.

Paul wrote the believers in Thessalonica concerning this issue. 1 Thessalonians 2:11–12:

11 As ye know how we exhorted and
comforted and charged every one of
you, as a father doth his children, 12 That

ye would walk worthy of God, who hath called you unto his kingdom and glory.

He exhorted, comforted, and charged his listeners. Something he can do for us today but only when we read and understand what he has written for us. Verses 13–14:

> 13 **For this cause also thank we God without ceasing, because, when ye received the word of God which ye heard of us, ye received it not as the word of men, but as it is in truth, <u>the word of God, which effectually worketh also in you that believe.</u> 14 For ye, brethren, became followers of the churches of God which in Judaea are in Christ Jesus: for ye also have suffered like things of your own countrymen, even as they have of the Jews:**

These believers received the Word of God as truth. That truth worked effectively in them because they received and accepted it as the truth. Above, the key word is *effectually* which means *in an effective manner, with great effect; completely*. It is about receiving and holding fast to the Word of Truth. By doing that, it works *effectually!*

Try saying this out loud, "I'm not what I was. I'm not that old man. I'm dead to sin." After we admit that, we must delve into God's Word. We must study it as we are doing right now. We must learn what the Word has to teach us. It is Paul who is teaching, but it is the Spirit Who, through the Word, *effectually* works in us because we believe. It is not about having head knowledge of the doctrines that Paul teaches. It is not simply knowing we are not under the Law. We must understand these *positional truths* that Paul teaches and embrace them *by faith.* We need to constantly affirm, "This is who I *really* am." When we are renewed by the Spirit in our mind, we are putting on the new man *in faith.* That is the only way we can live a victorious life *in Christ.* It is the *effectual* working of God's Word in us that brings about that *effect!*

Compare this to what most Christians attempt to do. Many choose some kind of self-improvement process. That is what most Christians today are doing. They are trying to improve themselves by *doing* good works to make up for their guilt. Then, they compare themselves to others to decide if they are *doing* enough. So, they are trying to make the old man better. Go to any Christian bookstore and you will find hundreds of books that tell Christians what they need *to do.* Most of them are about self-improvement. They may use Christian terminology to make it sound good. The books may sound biblical as they quote various verses out of context. Their purpose is to help Christians improve the old man. It does not work. Why? Remember, the old man is dead!

The old man is dead. We are now a new creature which was bought and paid for by the Blood of Christ. Praise God! He wants us to walk *by faith*. Again, how do we do that? We do that by trusting and studying His Word. When we do this, the Spirit can work within us *effectually* which means *completely*. (See Philippians 1:6.) This is not a self-improvement program. Forget all that foolishness.

We move on. Romans 6:7–8:

**7 For he that is dead is freed from sin. 8 Now if we be dead with Christ, we believe that we shall also live with him:**

It should be obvious. If we are dead, then we cannot sin. This makes us free from the power of sin. We are alive in Christ! Colossians 3:1–4:

**1 If ye then be risen with Christ, seek those things which are above, where Christ sitteth on the right hand of God. 2 Set your affection on things above, not**

on things on the earth. 3 For ye are dead, and your life is hid with Christ in God. 4 When Christ, who is our life, shall appear, then shall ye also appear with him in glory.

These are two great verses in Scripture that inspire us towards that *effectual* change. It is, again, talking about our present position *in Christ*. There is also a bonus reference to the Rapture, which is *the glory of God* in which we hope. As far as God is concerned, we are already risen *in Christ!* Knowing this, we are to set our affections on things above. This is another point on how to deal with sin. If our affections are set on things above, then we cannot set them on earthly things. Our life is now in Christ. When Christ appears and takes us unto Himself, then shall we also appear with Him in glory. I believe the above verses will give us a better understanding of Romans 6.

Let us go to Romans 6:9–10:

9 Knowing that Christ being raised from the dead dieth no more; death hath no more dominion over him. 10 For in that he died, he died unto sin once: but in that he liveth, he liveth unto God.

Since Christ is sinless and perfect, the grave could

not contain Him. Death had no hold over Him. He died once for us and He will never die again. 2 Corinthians 5:14–15:

> 14 **For the love of Christ constraineth us; because we thus judge, that if one died for all, then were all dead: 15 And that he died for all, that they which live should not henceforth live unto themselves, but unto him which died for them, and rose again.**

Christ died for all. So, those who live should no longer live for themselves. Instead, they should live for Him Who died for them. We continue. Verses 16–17:

> 16 **Wherefore henceforth know we no man after the flesh: yea, though we have known Christ after the flesh, yet now henceforth know we him no more. 17 Therefore if any man be in Christ, he is a new creature: old things are passed away; behold, all things are become new.**

We are not like those who were written about in the Gospels of Matthew, Mark, Luke, and John. They knew Christ in the *flesh*. However, we know

Christ through *faith*. In the past, there were only Jews and Gentiles (non-Jews). Today, there is something new under the sun. The Body of Christ is neither Jew nor Gentile. It is a new creation. No longer under the Law , but under grace. For this reason, Paul writes that the old system of the Law has passed away. The division between the Jews and Gentiles is taken away in the Body of Christ. All things are new. Everything God is doing for the Body of Christ in this Dispensation of Grace is new. There was never a time in the past when someone had Christ living *in them*. His Spirit dwells *in them*. There was never a time in the past when the Holy Spirit baptized a believer *into Christ*. Verses 18–21:

18 **And all things are of God, who hath reconciled us to himself by Jesus Christ, and hath given to us the ministry of reconciliation; 19 To wit, that God was in Christ, reconciling the world unto himself, not imputing their trespasses unto them; and hath committed unto us the word of reconciliation.**

20 **Now then we are ambassadors for Christ, as though God did beseech you by us: we pray you in Christ's stead, be ye reconciled to God. 21 For he hath made him to be sin for us, who knew no**

sin; that we might be made the right-eousness of God in him.

We read this to get to this point: the reason Christ died was to become sin for us. He took our place. As His ambassadors, He has given us the ministry of sharing the message of this reconciliation. Look at Revelation 1:18:

> 18 I am he that liveth, and was dead; and, behold, I am alive for evermore, Amen; and have the keys of hell and of death.

It is symbolic when Christ says He has "the keys of hell and of death." He is the One Who will judge the living and the dead.

We continue. Romans 6:11:

> 11 Likewise reckon ye also yourselves to be dead indeed unto sin, but alive unto God through Jesus Christ our Lord.

This is the conclusion of the preceding verses. We are now dead to sin and alive in Jesus Christ. Verses 12–14:

> 12 Let not sin therefore reign in your mortal body, that ye should obey it in

the lusts thereof. 13 Neither yield ye your members as instruments of unrighteousness unto sin: but yield yourselves unto God, as those that are alive from the dead, and your members as instruments of righteousness unto God. 14 For sin shall not have dominion over you: for <u>ye are not under the law, but under grace</u>.

Above, the word *reign* means to *rule or have dominion over* us. We are not to allow sin to rule over us in our mortal bodies. Why? It is because we are no longer under the Law. We are under grace. So, how are we to accomplish this? How can we prevent sin from reigning in our mortal bodies? How do we prevent our bodies from being used for unrighteousness?

To answer these questions, we will look at what is called the *replacement principle*. You will see what I mean by that in just a moment. We find our answers in Scripture. Galatians 5:16–18:

16 This I say then, Walk in the Spirit, and ye shall not fulfil the lust of the flesh. 17 For the flesh lusteth against the Spirit, and the Spirit against the flesh: and these are contrary the one to the other: so that ye cannot do the things

**that ye would. 18 But if ye be led of the Spirit, ye are not under the law.**

That is what I mean by the *replacement principle*. If we walk in the Spirit, then we will not chase the desires of the flesh. If we are led by the Spirit, we are no longer under the Law. Paul makes this important point. Many Christians try to use the Law as their guide for living. They think if they live the kind of life God wants, then they will please Him. By turning to the Law, they believe that this is what will keep them from sin. That approach is doomed to fail. Why? It is because the purpose of the Law is to condemn those who fail to be perfect. However, if they walk in the Spirit, they will not fulfill the lust of their flesh. That is the *replacement principle*.

One might ask, "What does it mean to walk in the spirit?" If we are walking in the Spirit, then we are studying our Bible, talking with God, and sharing the Gospel of Grace with others. In other words, we are busy doing things that have an eternal purpose. When we focus on spiritual things, then we are walking in the Spirit. Consider, again, Colossians 3:1–2:

**1 If ye then be risen with Christ, <u>seek those things which are above</u>, where Christ sitteth on the right hand of God.**

**2 Set your affection on things above, not on things on the earth.**

It is like looking up and looking down. We cannot do both at the same time. It is impossible. What we set our mind on and what we focus on pushes everything else out!

In order to walk in the Spirit by using the *replacement principal*, we must focus on spiritual things. We do this by focusing on the Word of God. Remember, Jesus Christ is the Word of God. When we spend time in the Word every day, we are renewing our mind by having the mind of Christ. It pushes out the other things. What we set our affections on is what we are going to be focused on. When we are focused on the Word, these other things will have no place in our thoughts. Sin will not find a place in our life. That is the idea I call the *replacement principle*. Repeat after me, "For sin shall not have dominion over you: for ye are not under the law, but under grace" (Rom. 6:14).

The purpose of the Law was to point out and expose sin. The Law condemns us and causes us to focus on sin without any remedy for it. There is a connection between sin and the Law. We have this sin nature with which we were born. Many try to deal with their sin nature through the Law. Yet, it causes people to focus on sin. When we are preoccupied with sin, there is no way of dealing with it. Paul addresses this very issue himself. He is the man who is trying to be spiritual. Romans 7:24:

> 24 O wretched man that I am! who shall deliver me from the body of this death?

He then asks the question, "Who shall deliver me from the body of this death?" Verse 25:

> 25 I thank God through Jesus Christ our Lord. So then with the mind I myself serve the law of God; but with the flesh the law of sin.

What we have is a *dichotomy* within us. A *dichotomy* means *a division into two parts*. So, with the renewing of our mind, we serve the Law of God. However, with our flesh we serve the Law of sin. Romans 8:1–4:

> 1 There is therefore now no condemnation to them which are in Christ Jesus, who walk not after the flesh, but after the Spirit. 2 For the law of the Spirit of life in Christ Jesus hath made me free from the law of sin and death. 3 For what the law could not do, in that it was

**weak through the flesh, God sending his own Son in the likeness of sinful flesh, and for sin, condemned sin in the flesh: 4 That the righteousness of the law might be fulfilled in us, who walk not after the flesh, but after the Spirit.**

The following verses outline the concept of the *replacement principle*. Verses 5-6:

**5 For they that are after the flesh do mind the things of the flesh; but they that are after the Spirit the things of the Spirit. 6 For to be carnally minded is death; but to be spiritually minded is life and peace.**

To what is Paul referring? The word *after* is used twice in the above verses: *after the flesh* and *after the spirit*. This is not referring to an order of time but the object being pursued, which is consistent with our primary focus. An example would be, "That dog was after our cat again today." This would mean that the dog was pursuing and focused on catching the cat. When we focus on or pursue the things pertaining to the flesh which is carnal, that ends in death. However, when we put our efforts and focus on pursuing the things of the Spirit, that brings life and peace. Paul goes on to talk about how we cannot be condemned when we walk *in the Spirit.* Once we realize we are a new creature in Christ and, as that singular truth affects us, we have a continual renewing of our mind. This will ultimately affect our behavior. That is what it means *to walk after the Spirit.*

Let us continue. Romans 6:15–16:

**15 What then? shall we sin, because we are not under the law, but under grace? God forbid. 16 Know ye not, that to whom ye yield yourselves servants to obey, his servants ye are to whom ye obey; whether of sin unto death, or of obedience unto righteousness?**

For those of us that are part of what is sometimes referred to as the *grace movement,* we are often accused of being *antinomian* or *against the Law.* They accuse us of believing we can do anything we want and it is okay, but that is not what Paul is talking about here. Paul is talking about the fact that it is *grace* that gives us the power to live our lives approved by Him; not by the Law.

Paul anticipated people asking, "What then? Shall we go on sinning because we are not under the Law, but under grace?" His immediate response is, "God forbid!" Positionally, we are already dead, buried, and resurrected with Christ. Positionally, we are a new creature in Christ. We are complete in Christ. We have His righteousness imputed to us. However, if we continue to serve sin, then it is still our master. That makes sense. From a practical standpoint, to whatever we are a slave, that is our master. Sin leads to death. Obedience leads to righteousness. With one choice the wages or results are death. With the other choice, the wages or reward is life.

When we sin as a believer, as a member of the Body of Christ, that is an action void of any spiritual life. Functionally, that is death. This does not mean that God is going to take away our salvation. However, when we sin as a believer, functionally, that is death. It is void of any life. As Grace Believers, we must focus on believing Paul's doctrine. In other words, we must have faith in these principles which are, in effect, an expression of Christ's righteousness. When we try to keep the Law, it is not an expression of Christ's righteousness. It is an expression of our own self-righteousness.

We continue. Verses 17–18:

**17 But God be thanked, that ye were the servants of sin, but ye have obeyed from the heart that form of doctrine**

**which was delivered you. 18 Being then made free from sin, ye became the servants of righteousness.**

Notice the past tense of the verbs used here. We *were* servants of sin and we *have obeyed* from the heart the doctrines that Christ revealed to Paul. By doing this, we are being made free from sin and became servants of righteousness. We are already there. This obedience was from the heart. Why? It was because it was a genuine acceptance of the doctrine received from Paul. What he delivered he had also received! Can you think of another place in the Bible where Paul talks about delivering something he had received? He delivered the Gospel of Grace. 1 Corinthians 15:3–4:

> **3 For I delivered unto you first of all that which I also received, how [1] that Christ died for our sins according to the scriptures; 4 And [2] that he was buried, and [3] that he rose again the third day according to the scriptures:**

Paul delivered what he received from Christ. When we obey the doctrine that Paul preached, Who are we really obeying? We are obeying Christ. By wholeheartedly believing and obeying Paul's teaching, we are acting upon our faith in God's Word. We are putting the Gospel of Grace into action.

We continue. Romans 6:19–20:

> 19 I speak after the manner of men be-
> cause of the infirmity of your flesh: for
> as ye have yielded your members serv-
> ants to uncleanness and to iniquity unto
> iniquity; even so now yield your mem-
> bers servants to righteousness unto ho-
> liness. 20 For when ye were the servants
> of sin, ye were free from righteousness.

Where we once yielded to the flesh which produced
iniquity, we now yield to righteousness which produces holiness. Verses 21–22:

> 21 What fruit had ye then in those things
> whereof ye are now ashamed? for the
> end of those things is death. 22 But now
> being made free from sin, and become
> servants to God, ye have your fruit unto
> holiness, and the end everlasting life.

The fruit or results of sinning in the past led to
death. Now, we are no longer under sin and no
longer its slave. We are free. The results or the fruit
is holiness and eternal life. We all know the things
we did before we were saved by God's grace; we are

ashamed of them. Our conscience told us that we were sinners and we are ashamed. The result of those things is death. In other words, there was no spiritual life in those things. We were spiritually dead because sin always leads to death.

In the last verse of this chapter, Paul powerfully sums up both the problem and the solution. Verse 23:

**23 For the wages of sin is death; but the gift of God is eternal life through Jesus Christ our Lord.**

Wages or consequences are the results of an action. Here, Paul affirms that the wages of sin is death. Besides making us aware of the problem, he also tells us that God has provided the solution. Believing in the finished work of Jesus Christ, we have God's solution which leads to eternal life. And, better yet, it is available to all who believe!

# 12

Romans 7

Paul continues to build upon what he has taught so far. In this chapter, the theme is being dead to both the law and our sin nature. When we talk about the law, as it relates to the Gentiles, we are not talking about the *Mosaic Law*. The Gentiles were never under the *Mosaic Law* because God gave that covenant to Israel.

In Genesis, after God expelled Adam and Eve from the Garden of Eden, it was a new world. Since that time, God has instilled a conscience in every individual. This conscience in us is referred to as the *Moral Law*. The concept of right and wrong was written into everyone's heart to be their guide. When the Apostle Paul is talking to the Gentiles about the law, he is referring to this *Moral Law*. We can also call it the *Law of Conscience*. It is on this law that Paul will now focus.

We will start by looking back at Romans 2:12–16:

12 **For as many as have sinned without law shall also perish without law: and as many as have sinned in the law shall be judged by the law;** 13 **(For not the hearers of the law are just before God, but the doers of the law shall be justified.** 14 **For when the Gentiles, which have not the law, do by nature the things contained in the law, these, having not the law, are a law unto themselves:** 15 **Which shew the work of the law written in their hearts, their conscience also bearing witness, and their thoughts the mean while accusing or else excusing one another;)** 16 **In the day when God shall judge the secrets of men by Jesus Christ according to my gospel.**

The *Moral Law* is included in the Mosaic Law. The Jews had far greater requirements including ceremonial, sacrificial, and social laws. As Gentiles, it is the *Moral Law* to which our consciences bear witness.

We are going to learn something very important. In both Romans 7 and 8, Paul discloses principles concerning the interaction between the *sin nature* and the *Moral Law*. There are five of these laws. Only one of them is from the Law of Moses while the other four are like the law of gravity. We know that whatever goes up must come down. We will look at each of them individually in order to understand them.

Let us begin with a block of text and then we can discuss it. Romans 7:1–6:

> 1 **Know ye not, brethren, (for I speak to them that know the law,) how that the law hath dominion over a man as long as he liveth? 2 For the woman which hath an husband is bound by the law to her husband so long as he liveth; but if the husband be dead, she is loosed from the law of her husband.**
>
> 3 **So then if, while her husband liveth, she be married to another man, she shall be called an adulteress: but if her husband be dead, she is free from that law; so that she is no adulteress, though she be married to another man. 4 Wherefore, my brethren, ye also are become dead to the law by the body of Christ; that ye should be married to another,**

even to him who is raised from the dead, that we should bring forth fruit unto God.

5 For when we were in the flesh, the motions of sins, which were by the law, did work in our members to bring forth fruit unto death. 6 But now we are delivered from the law, that being dead wherein we were held; that we should serve in newness of spirit, and not in the oldness of the letter.

Here, Paul uses the word "brethren" because he is directing this point to the Jews saved by grace. He states that as long as they are alive, they are subject to the Law which means the *Mosaic Law*. He makes a comparison relative to them, again calling them "brethren," saying, "but now" we, as members of the Body of Christ, are dead to the Law in order to walk in newness of the Spirit.

We are going to get to the issue of the interaction between the *sin nature* and *the Law*. Verses 7–11:

7 What shall we say then? Is the law sin? God forbid. Nay, I had not known sin, but by the law: for I had not known lust, except the law had said, Thou shalt not

covet. 8 But sin, taking occasion by the commandment, wrought in me all manner of concupiscence. For without the law sin was dead.

9 For I was alive without the law once: but when the commandment came, sin revived, and I died. 10 And the commandment, which was ordained to life, I found to be unto death. 11 For sin, taking occasion by the commandment, deceived me, and by it slew me.

Paul tells us he did not know anything about sin until he learned the Law. He gives us the example of lust. We know that we are now delivered from the Law because we are dead to it. Being now dead to the law, we are to serve in newness of the Spirit which resides in us. We are no longer under the *letter* of the Law. Paul anticipated a question, "Is the Law sin?" and he answers this question, :God forbid!" The Law is not sin, but it reveals it.

We know the purpose of the Law was to expose and reveal sin in our lives. We can see this clearly in Romans 3:20:

20 Therefore by the deeds of the law there shall no flesh be justified in his

**sight: for by the law is the knowledge of sin.**

By the Law, we have the knowledge of sin. For our understanding, the Apostle Paul will go into greater detail about this issue in this chapter. We start by understanding that the Law makes us aware of the sin problem, but it does not provide the solution. It just makes us aware.

Think of the Law as a schoolmaster who teaches us. Galatians 3:24–25:

> **24 Wherefore the law was our schoolmaster to bring us unto Christ, that we might be justified by faith. 25 But after that faith is come, we are no longer under a schoolmaster.**

The point is this: Christ is the solution. The Law points out the problem. Christ is the solution to the problem. When we really understand what the Law is teaching us, we understand the destitute condition we are in. This should point us to Christ. It should point us to the Cross. If it does not, then something is wrong. It should never lead us to say, "Well, I just need to try harder to keep the Law. I just need to try harder to live up to that standard." If we do, that puts us on that religious treadmill that so many Christians are on today.

We continue. Romans 7:8:

**8 But sin, taking occasion by the commandment, wrought in me all manner of concupiscence. For without the law sin was dead.**

When Paul says *occasion*, he is talking about *opportunity*. He is saying sin takes the opportunity by the commandment, which is the Law, to create in me all sorts of *concupiscence*. What is this? *Concupiscence* is when our sinful desires become intensified because the Law tells us we cannot do something. It creates an intense desire in us to rebel against the Law.

Let me give an example. You are in a room. I come into this room with you, and I have a box in my hand. It is a closed box, and I hand you the box. I say to you, "I want you to guard this box and keep it safe. I will be back in an hour. You *must not* open this box. I will repeat myself. You *cannot* open this box while I am gone. I will be back in an hour to get my box. You *cannot* open the box. Do you understand? You are *not allowed* to open the box." What are you going to be thinking about the whole time I am gone? You are going to be thinking what is in the box, right? You will be really curious about what is in the box. Your desire to know what is in the box gets stronger the more you think about what is inside that box. Well, that is the idea. The word *concupiscence* means *the desire to break the commandments*. It becomes heightened and more intense because the Law is forbidding it. In fact, the more the Law says *thou shalt not,* the more we want to do what the Law forbids. Sin takes the opportunity because of the commandment to create in us all manner of desire to do exactly what the Law forbids. For without the Law, sin was dead. In other words, without the Law, there is no awareness of sin.

Here is another way to think about this. When we were a child or, for those of us who are familiar with small children, we know they are not aware of doing anything wrong until Mom and Dad gives them rules to obey. After that, the rules are to be obeyed because now they have knowledge of them. This gives us some kind of idea of what Paul is communicating here. Children do not know what is right or wrong until they are told; then they become aware of what is wrong. Verse 9:

> 9 **For I was alive without the law once: but when the commandment came, sin revived, and I died.**

Paul talks about his natural state when he was born. He was very much alive without the Law, before having any knowledge of it. If he had no knowledge of the Law, then he is not consciously thinking about right and wrong. He goes on to say that the Law showed him that he was really dead, deserving of death due to sin. An analogy would be this: Let us say someone is feeling as fit as a fiddle. He feels healthy. He feels strong. He is never sick. Everything physically seems to be going great. One day he goes to the doctor for his annual physical and the doctor says that he has bad news. He informs him that he has late-stage cancer. He responds, "But I have felt great. How can that be?" The doctor shows them the x-rays and, now, he knows something he did not know before. That is what Paul is saying here. The Law showed him his sin. He is now aware of his sin nature and of the sin that dwelled within him. Becoming aware of sin, he realizes the penalty of sin is death and he dies. The Law makes us aware of our sin. This is like the doctor who showed the patient his condition. Up until that point, he was unaware.

We continue. Verses 10–11:

10 **And the commandment, which was ordained to life, I found to be unto death. 11 For sin, taking occasion by the commandment, deceived me, and by it slew me.**

The commandment which is the Law was to bring life. However, instead of bringing life, it brought death. What does this mean? To answer that, we need to look at Deuteronomy 30:15–16:

> 15 **See, I have set before thee this day life and good, and death and evil; 16 In that I command thee this day to love the LORD thy God, to walk in his ways, and to keep his commandments and his statutes and his judgments, that thou mayest live and multiply: and the LORD thy God shall bless thee in the land whither thou goest to possess it.**

The Law was to set before the people life and good as well as death and evil. We continue. Verse 19:

> 19 **I call heaven and earth to record this day against you, that <u>I have set before you life and death, blessing and cursing</u>: <u>therefore choose life</u>, that both thou and thy seed may live:**

God has given them His commandments and now they have a choice between life and death. He urges them to "choose life." If they do not, they will die. The Law was enacted to bring life. Yet, because of his fallen nature, Paul found the Law brought death.

Paul realized he could not keep the Law. No one can keep the Law. Sin took the opportunity and used the Law. Paul was deceived into trying to keep the Law. Then, he realized its purpose. It showed him his sin nature and, with that knowledge, he died. Ephesians 2:1:

> 1 **And you hath he quickened, who were dead in trespasses and sins;**

Because of sin, we are dead. The Law does not discriminate and, therefore, it slew Paul also. Once he thought he was alive, but then he realized, because of the Law, he was dead.

Here is another reference to consider. Matthew 8: 21–22:

> 21 **And another of his disciples said unto him, Lord, suffer [allow] me first to go and bury my father.** 22 **But Jesus said unto him, Follow me; and let the dead bury their dead.**

This follower wants to go with Jesus, but he wants to first bury his father who had died. Jesus responds, "let the dead bury their dead." He was speaking about those who were not *physically* dead, but *spiritually* dead.

We move on. Romans 7:12–14:

**12 Wherefore the law is holy, and the commandment holy, and just, and good. 13 Was then that which is good made death unto me? God forbid. But sin, that it might appear sin, working death in me by that which is good; that sin by the commandment might become exceeding sinful. 14 For we know that the law is spiritual: but I am carnal, sold under sin.**

We need to look at these three verses together as a group. Regarding the Law, Paul says it is holy, it is just, it is good, and it is spiritual. It is all of this because it came from God, right? God gave us His standard for perfection. It is His standard for righteousness. It is His standard for holiness. It reveals God's character and establishes His standards. It also reveals the fact that we cannot meet those standards through striving. We cannot keep His standard. The Law shows how carnal and helpless we are. Paul uses a phrase to describe his state. He says he was "carnal" and "sold under sin." We are all slaves to sin and the Law is our master.

In 2 Kings, we find some relevant history about Israel. 2 Kings 17:16–17:

**16 And they left all the commandments of the LORD their God, and made them molten images, even two calves, and made a grove, and worshipped all the host of heaven, and served Baal. 17 And they caused their sons and their daughters to pass through the fire, and used divination and enchantments, and sold themselves to do evil in the sight of the LORD, to provoke him to anger.**

They had abandoned all the commandments. They had rejected the Law and "sold themselves to do evil in the sight of the Lord." They did this on purpose to provoke the Lord God to anger. The word *sold* is used in the context of "being totally given over" to something. Paul uses the same concept in Romans 7:14. He uses *sold under sin* which means *to be dominated or completely controlled by sin*. Paul is the pattern we are to follow and he acknowledges that his *sin nature* had dominion over him.

There are some Christians that hold to a belief that Romans 7 is talking about a lost person who is trying to obey God's Law. They teach that the reason they cannot obey God's Law is because they are lost. That is not true whatsoever. In Romans 7, Paul is discussing those who are saved and struggling with their sin nature. Although they are saved by grace through faith, they still have a sin nature warring against their spirit. This applies to all of us who are saved. Now, with that said, let us continue. Romans 7:15–20:

> 15 For that which I do I allow not: for what I would, that do I not; but what I hate, that do I. 16 If then I do that which I would not, I consent unto the law that it is good. 17 Now then it is no more I that do it, but sin [the sin nature] that dwelleth in me. 18 For I know that in me (that is, in my flesh,) dwelleth no good thing: for to will is present with me; but how to perform that which is good I find not. 19 For the good that I would I do not: but the evil which I would not, that I do. 20 Now if I do that I would not, it is no more I that do it, but sin [the sin nature] that dwelleth in me.

Remember, Paul is talking about the interaction between the *sin nature* and the *Moral Law* of God. Everyone who is saved still has this *sin nature*. We have this as part of our human nature. However, we have a conscience, and our conscience tells us there is right and wrong. Here, Paul is speaking of the sin that dwells within him; he is speaking of his own *sin nature*. He says that in his *flesh* there is nothing good.

He admits that the good that he would choose to do, he does not; while the evil that he would not choose to do, he does. All of this is because of the *sin nature* that dwells in him. Paul continues. Verse 21:

> 21 **I find then a law, that, when I would do good, evil is present with me.**

Now, we are going to talk about these biblical principles I mentioned at the beginning of this chapter. We all know that we have a *sin nature* that constantly seeks to rebel against God's Law. At the same time, we have a conscience that bears witness to the *Moral Law* that tells us what is right and wrong. That conscience we have learned is the *Moral Law* or *Law of Conscience*. It was written in our hearts when we were born. These points are so important that they need repeating. Let us return to Romans 2:14–15:

> 14 **For when the Gentiles, which have not the law, do by nature the things contained in the law, these, having not the law, are a law unto themselves: 15 Which shew the work of the law written in their hearts, their conscience also bearing witness, and their thoughts the mean while accusing or else excusing one another;)**

The Gentiles were never given the Law of Moses which was a covenant with the Jews. However, when they do by *sin nature* that which is against their conscience which is written in their heart also, they break the *Moral Law*. Even though Gentiles were not given the *Mosaic Law*, their consciences bear witness to the *Moral Law* which God gave everyone. This conscience they apply by either accusing or excusing one another. What is Paul saying here? It is very simple. Everyone, whether they are saved, unsaved, Jew, or Gentile, has a conscience. With this inherent knowledge of right and wrong, we use it to either excuse or accuse one another for various actions. We base this solely upon the Law of Conscience.

As we look at the biblical principles that Paul is teaching, we will break it down in more detail. Romans 7:22:

**22 For I delight in the law of God after the inward man:**

Paul delights in this inherent *Moral Law* of God which is the God-given conscience. The inner man experiences a warring within himself. Remember, these are principles. We are not talking about the Law of Moses. We are talking about these *principles of conscience.* There is a warring or battle raging within us. It is between our *sin nature* and our *con-*

*science*. It attempts to confuse what is right and wrong. Here is a principal, a fact. As fallen children of Adam, sin is in our nature. Let us read this once more. Romans 7:14–15:

> **14 For we know that the law is spiritual: but I am carnal, sold under sin. 15 For that which I do I allow not: for what I would, that do I not; but what I hate, that do I.**

Understanding this constant warring going on within us does explain a lot. How can we handle this?

There are four principles. The first principle is acknowledging the *Moral Law* of God. This is what Paul is talking about when he wrote, "For I delight in the Law of God after the inward man" (v. 22). This inherent *Moral Law* is our conscience. The second principle is the indwelling of sin. It is referred to as our fallen nature or the *sin nature*. Paul continues, "In my flesh dwelleth no good thing" (v. 18). It acknowledges our helplessness. The third principle is our change of attitude which I call the *renewing of the mind*. This occurs when we become aware of the Law and understand that the consequence of breaking the law is death. When Paul writes "I delight in the Law of God after the inward man," (v. 22) he is referring to his renewed mind. With salvation there is a change in the inner man. With his renewed mind, Paul now delights in what is good and what is right. Verse 23:

> 23 **But I see another law in my members, warring against the law of my mind, and bringing me into captivity to the law of sin which is in my members.**

Here, the word *members* refers to the *flesh*. Paul calls this flesh "a wretched man." Verse 24:

> 24 **O wretched man that I am! who shall deliver me from the body of this death?**

These members to which Paul refers are parts of the body. They war against his mind affecting his ability to choose right from wrong. The words "body of this death" are just another way of saying his *flesh* which is still under his old sin nature. How can he escape? Who will save him from this "body of death" that does not want to do right? The flesh cannot do anything right because it is a slave or captive to sin. Since we cannot save ourselves, Paul asks, "who shall deliver me from the body of this death?" (v. 24). Verse 25:

> 25 **I thank God through Jesus Christ our**

**Lord. So then with the mind I myself serve the law of God; but with the flesh the law of sin.**

This internal conflict is between our sin nature and our conscience. As believers, we are a new creation in Christ. Yet, we struggle to do good and cannot. The flesh works to do those things which are contrary to God. What are these works of the flesh? Paul provides us with a list in Galatians 5:19–21:

> 19 **Now the works of the flesh are manifest, which are these; Adultery, fornication, uncleanness, lasciviousness, 20 Idolatry, witchcraft, hatred, variance, emula-tions, wrath, strife, seditions, heresies, 21 Envyings, murders, drunkenness, revellings, and such like: of the which I tell you before, as I have also told you in time past, that they which do such things shall not inherit the kingdom of God.**

These are the evil acts which the flesh works to do.

So, then, what is the solution? In the next chapter, our study of these principles continues. There, we will find the solution to this predicament.

220

# 13

## Romans 8 (Part I)

In this chapter, Paul answers a lot of questions: "How do we serve God?," "How do we please God?," and, "How do we glorify God in our lives?" We already learned that we cannot do this by keeping the Law. Besides, we are no longer under the Law. We learned that it is impossible to keep the Law because our flesh works against us. Therefore, we must serve God by walking according to the Spirit. The moment we believed the gospel, spiritually, we went from being "in the flesh" to being "in the Spirit." Now, "being in the Spirit," we are free from the law of sin and death. Now, being "in Christ," our life is in Him. Therefore, we are to walk "in the Spirit."

Paul explained the conflict we have between our sin nature and our consciousness of right and wrong. We have been baptized into Christ's death and raised to walk in newness of life. We have the power through the Holy Spirit to choose not to sin. By faith, we reckon ourselves to be dead unto sin and alive unto God. We need to continually claim our new identity in Christ. We have a new purpose and have the power to choose to keep sin out of our lives. This supersedes the struggle between the sin nature and conscience. All we have to do is walk in the Spirit. One could ask, "But how do I walk in the Spirit?" Great question! Paul will answer that question for us.

So far, we have learned three biblical principles. Let us take a moment to briefly recall them. First, we were delivered from the bondage of the Law. Second, we learned that we cannot keep the Law because of our sin nature. Third, at salvation, our inward man is changed. The renewing of our minds through His Word allows us to delight in God's laws. This gives us the ability to be victorious over sin because of the renewing of our minds. Romans 7 ended with this. Romans 7: 24–25:

> 24 **O wretched man that I am! who shall deliver me from the body of this death? 25 I thank God through Jesus Christ our Lord. So then with the mind I myself serve the law of God; but with the flesh the law of sin.**

Paul begins Romans 8 with the word *therefore*. He comes to a conclusion based upon what he has presented so far. Romans 8:1:

**1 There is therefore now no condemnation to them which are in Christ Jesus, who walk not after the flesh, but after the Spirit.**

Here we are introduced to the fourth biblical principle. As a result of the first three, Paul concludes, there is "now no condemnation" to those who are "in Christ Jesus." In other words, the law condemns us, but "in Christ Jesus" there is no condemnation. Verse 2:

**2 For the law of the Spirit of life in Christ Jesus hath made me free from the law of sin and death.**

This brings us to our fifth principle. Paul talks about the fact that death is inevitable because of our sin nature. Everyone will die physically unless they are raptured while they are alive at His Calling. Those who die without believing the gospel will not only die but end up in the Lake of Fire. Death is the consequence of sin. (See Romans 6:23.) This is called the principle of sin and death.

There is another biblical principle that countermands the principle of sin and death. That is the principle of the spirit of life in Christ Jesus. This frees those who believe the Gospel of Grace from the principle of sin and death. Yes, we will physically die, but death cannot hold us because we are safe "in Christ." There is no condemnation for those who have the righteousness of Christ. God has imputed His Son's righteousness to us. The principle of the spirit of life in Christ has made us free from the principle of sin and death. Our new life is "in Christ."

Therefore, we can now walk in the Spirit. Verses 3–8:

> 3 For what the law could not do, in that it was weak through the flesh, God sending his own Son in the likeness of sinful flesh, and for sin, condemned sin in the flesh: 4 That the righteousness of the law might be fulfilled in us, who walk not after the flesh, but after the Spirit. 5 For they that are after the flesh do mind the things of the flesh; but they that are after the Spirit the things of the Spirit. 6 For to be carnally minded is death; but to be spiritually minded is life and peace. 7 Because the carnal mind is enmity against God: for it is not

**subject to the law of God, neither indeed can be. 8 So then they that are in the flesh cannot please God.**

People who are fleshly-minded concern themselves with fleshly things which they find enticing due to the "sin nature." Those who set their minds on spiritual things will concern themselves with spiritual matters. They see things from God's perspective. The carnal or fleshly mind is at enmity with God. Those that operate in the flesh cannot please God.

Paul continues with verses 9–11:

**9 But ye are not in the flesh, but in the Spirit, if so be that the Spirit of God dwell in you. Now if any man have not the Spirit of Christ, he is none of his. 10 And if Christ be in you, the body is dead because of sin; but the Spirit is life because of righteousness. 11 But if the Spirit of him that raised up Jesus from the dead dwell in you, he that raised up Christ from the dead shall also quicken your mortal bodies by his Spirit that dwelleth in you.**

In verse 9 above, Paul begins with the word "but." This signals that what follows is contrary or an exception to what preceded. Remember that Paul teaches that the law or principle of the spirit and life has made him free from this principle of sin and death. Then, he begins to discuss the believer's service. That is what it means to be "walking after the Spirit." If we walk after the Spirit, then we can serve God and it pleases Him. However, if we walk after the flesh, then we are condemned.

When people see that word *condemned,* they usually ask, "Is Paul talking about me? Is this about me losing my salvation?" Many Christians get this idea because of how they interpret Scripture. We are studying Scripture by rightly dividing the Word of Truth. (See 2 Timothy 2:15.) We follow Paul's instruction concerning the interpretation of Scripture. The word *condemnation* is used in different contexts within Scripture. Here are a few examples. John 3:18–19:

> 18 **He that believeth on him is not condemned: but he that believeth not is condemned already, because he hath not believed in the name of the only begotten Son of God. 19 And this is the condemnation, that light is come into the world, and men loved darkness rather than light, because their deeds were evil.**

Above, the *condemnation* is coming from God for not believing in His Son. This *condemnation* results in eternal damnation.

Here is another way that *condemnation* is used in Scripture. Paul is discussing how believers on Corinth were conducting themselves during the Lord's Supper. 1 Corinthians 11:32–34:

> 32 **But when we are judged, we are chastened of the Lord, that we should not be condemned with the world.** 33 **Wherefore, my brethren, when ye come together to eat, tarry [wait for] one for another.** 34 **And if any man hunger, let him eat at home; that ye come not together unto condemnation. And the rest will I set in order when I come.**

This is *condemnation* from our behavior. This *condemnation* is judgment that comes from the world who are observing their behavior. No one is losing their salvation because the Corinthians were already saved by grace.

Let us also take a look at Titus 3:10–11:

> 10 **A man that is an heretick [heretic] after the first and second admonition**

reject; 11 **Knowing that he that is such is subverted, and sinneth, being condemned of himself.**

A heretic condemns himself because he believes bad doctrine or heresy. We always need to check the context in which words are used. Finally, when it comes to *condemnation*, remember this. Romans 8:1:

> 1 **There is therefore now no condemnation to them which are in Christ Jesus, who walk not after the flesh, but after the Spirit.**

Everything that is done in the flesh will be condemned. Who condemns us? Interestingly, we condemn ourselves. We can no longer be condemned. We have been set free. Why? It is because we are spiritually "in Christ Jesus."

Paul continues. Verse 3:

> 3 **For what the law could not do, in that it was weak through the flesh, God sending his own Son in the likeness of sinful flesh, and for sin, condemned sin in the flesh:**

What Christ did on the cross for us took care of our

sin issue. Our sin no longer condemns us. We are *in Christ* with His righteousness imputed to us. Verse 4:

**4 That the righteousness of the law might be fulfilled in us, who walk not after the flesh, but after the Spirit.**

When Paul says, "*the righteousness of the Law*," he is not talking about the Law itself. We already learned that we are not under the Law. We cannot serve God by keeping the Law whose purpose is only to condemn us. Trying to keep the Law would be following after the flesh. What does Paul mean by "the righteousness of the Law" might be fulfilled in us?

Consider this. Romans 13:8–10:

**8 Owe no man any thing, but to love one another: for he that loveth another hath fulfilled the law. 9 For this, Thou shalt not commit adultery, Thou shalt not kill, Thou shalt not steal, Thou shalt not bear false witness, Thou shalt not covet; and if there be any other commandment, it is briefly comprehended in this saying, namely, Thou shalt love thy neighbour as thyself. 10 Love worketh no ill to his neighbour: therefore love is the fulfilling of the law.**

We see that the *Moral Law* is the same as the *Law of Conscience*. It is love that fulfills the Law! What is the first fruit of the Holy Spirit? Love! How do we show love to our brothers and sisters in Christ and to our neighbors? We choose not to work any ill against them. That is the expression of love and it fulfills the Law. When we walk after the Spirit, we will not work any ill towards another.

Consider what Paul wrote to the believers in Galatia. Galatians 5:13–14:

> 13 **For, brethren, ye have been called unto liberty; only use not liberty for an occasion to the flesh, but by love serve one another. 14 For all the law is fulfilled in one word, even in this; Thou shalt love thy neighbour as thyself.**

In both Romans and Galatians, Paul is communicating that, when we walk after the Spirit, we fulfill the Law. How do we love our brothers and sisters in Christ and our neighbors? We do them no harm. The way we do that is by loving them. We express love by not committing adultery, fornication, or lying. We do not cheat or steal. We hurt other people when we sin. When we do those things, we are not showing love. Instead, we are being selfish and self-centered because we do not care how our actions affect others.

Most importantly, when we show love, we are fulfilling the Law.

Let us go back to Romans 8:4–5:

**4 That the righteousness of the law might be fulfilled in us, who walk not after the flesh, but after the Spirit. 5 For they that are after the flesh do mind the things of the flesh; but they that are after the Spirit the things of the Spirit.**

Here is an important point. Those who follow the flesh concentrate on the things of the flesh. Keep this in mind. Jeremiah 17: 9–10:

**9 The heart is deceitful above all things, and desperately wicked: who can know it? 10 I the LORD search the heart, I try the reins, even to give every man according to his ways, and according to the fruit of his doings.**

We see that "they that are after the flesh do mind the things of the flesh; but they that are after the Spirit the things of the Spirit" (v. 8:5). So, anything that is after the flesh is based upon the deceitfulness of the heart which is the wickedness of the heart. However, those that follow the Spirit are mindful of the things of the spirit. It all begins in the mind. Let us look back. Romans 7:21–23:

> 21 I find then a law, that, when I would do good, evil is present with me. 22 For I delight in the law of God after the inward man: 23 But I see another law in my members, warring against the law of my mind, and bringing me into captivity to the law of sin which is in my members.

The new man delights in the Law, but the old man is warring against it. Why is our old man constantly warring against the new man?

For the answer to this question, look at Ephesians 2: 1–3:

> 1 And you hath he quickened, who were dead in trespasses and sins; 2 Wherein in time past ye walked according to the course of this world, according to the prince of the power of the air, the spirit that now worketh in the children of disobedience: 3 Among whom also we all had our conversation in times past in the lusts of our flesh, fulfilling the desires of the flesh and of the mind; and were by nature the children of wrath,

**even as others.**

We read that we "were dead in trespasses and sins" and "fulfilling the desires of the flesh and of the mind." Paul uses the phrase *the course of this world.* His explanation gives us the understanding that means *according to the standards of this world.* This world is under the control of the "prince of the power of the air" and "the spirit that now worketh in the children of disobedience."

Paul elaborates on our spiritual enemy. Ephesians 6:12:

> 12 **For we wrestle not against flesh and blood, but against principalities, against powers, against the rulers of the darkness of this world, against spiritual wickedness in high places.**

Also in verse 3, he used the word *conversation* which means *manner of living* or *lifestyle.* Our manner of living was fulfilling the desires of our flesh and of our mind. Remember: it always begins in the mind. It is our mind that controls everything. Our mind controls our actions, our attitudes, and what we are thinking. Once we believe the gospel and the Spirit of God indwells in us, we become new creatures in Christ. However, the old man who is corrupt still remains in us. Ephesians 4:17:

> 17 **This I say therefore, and testify in the Lord, that ye henceforth walk not as other Gentiles walk, in the vanity of their mind,**

Paul tells us that we are *not* to walk in the vanity of our mind. We do this by default. We do not automatically walk after the Spirit, but will, by default, walk after the flesh. This is how unsaved Gentiles walk – in the vanity of their own mind.

He continues. Verses 18–21:

> 18 **Having the understanding darkened, being alienated from the life of God through the ignorance that is in them, because of the blindness of their heart: 19 Who being past feeling have given themselves over unto lasciviousness, to work all uncleanness with greediness. 20 But ye have not so learned Christ; 21 If so be that ye have heard him, and have been taught by him, as the truth is in Jesus:**

Paul refers to what we just learned. This concerns the mind of Christ, the heart of Christ, the purpose of

Christ, and our position "in Christ." Sins such as lasciviousness, uncleanness, and greediness were not learned from Christ. When we are taught by Christ, we are taught the Truth. Verses 22–24:

> **22 That ye put off concerning the former conversation the old man, which is corrupt according to the deceitful lusts; 23 And be renewed in the spirit of your mind; 24 And that ye put on the new man, which after God is created in righteousness and true holiness.**

We know the truth from God's Word. Those saved by grace are to put off our former lifestyle or manner of living. Then, we are to replace it through "the renewing of our mind." In other words, we need to make a conscious choice. We need to continually choose to renew our mind. It is a choice. Otherwise, we will walk in the vanity of our own thoughts. Again, we need to make a conscious effort to change our thinking. Now, how does that work exactly?

It is really very simple. We cannot walk after the Spirit without the renewing of our mind. This is accomplished *by faith*. We need to embrace God's words, *by faith*, given to us by Paul. We must *believe* who we are in Christ and, *by faith*, claim that truth. We must admit, "Yes. I am dead to sin and alive unto

God." This *is* the changing of our mind. Then, it becomes about focusing our desires and our thoughts. Colossians 3:1–3:

> 1 **If ye then be risen with Christ, seek those things which are above, where Christ sitteth on the right hand of God.** 2 <u>**Set your affection on things above, not on things on the earth.**</u> 3 <u>**For ye are dead, and your life is hid with Christ in God.**</u>

We must consider our present position. It states that we are *positionally* in Christ. And, where is He at present? He is seated at the right hand of God the Father in heaven. Think about this. We are *positionally* in Christ. We need to believe and hold on to this. In the armor of God, He gives us a helmet to protect our hope of salvation. (See Ephesians 6:17 and 1 Thessalonians 5:8.) We must never forget it! Then, keeping this knowledge, we will set our affections on the things above which are the teachings of God's Word. That is our "renewing of the mind."

In chapter 11, I referred to something I called the "replacement principle." If we "replace" our thoughts with the truth from the Word of God and think about who we are in Christ, then we cannot be carnally-minded. For we cannot be both spiritually-minded and carnally-minded at the same time.

Therefore, if we are spiritually-minded by focusing on God's Word, then we are walking after the Spirit. This is exactly how it works!

Let us repeat Romans 8:5:

**5 For they that are after the flesh do mind the things of the flesh; but they that are after the Spirit the things of the Spirit.**

We cannot walk after the Spirit unless we are spiritually-minded. The other alternative, being carnally-minded, results in death. What is Paul saying here? If we think about it for a minute, what is the opposite of life? The answer is death, right? If we choose to exercise our free will, we can walk in newness of life. To do that, we need to walk after the Spirit, right? However, if we are being carnally-minded, then we have the absence of spiritual life, even though we are a saved person. There is the absence of spiritual life. Do not let religion confuse this issue. Remember this: if we believed the gospel, then we are now complete in Christ. We were sealed unto the day of redemption. Nothing can change that. Nothing. However, being carnally-minded means that there is an absence of spiritual life. For the Spirit of God to work in our life, we have to be spiritually-minded.

Here we see it again in Paul's words. Verses 6–8:

> 6 **For to be carnally minded is death; but to be spiritually minded is life and peace.** 7 **Because the carnal mind is enmity against God: for it is not subject to the law of God, neither indeed can be.** 8 **So then they that are in the flesh cannot please God.**

The reward for being spiritually-minded is life and peace. However, when we are carnally-minded, it does not work. There is no rest. If believers who have been saved by grace become carnally-minded, there is stress, anguish, and disruption in their spiritual life. There is no peace. This is because the carnally-minded are operating at enmity with God. The word *enmity* means *in a state of opposition*. Therefore, the carnally-minded are in a state of opposing God. With all that Christ has done for us, do we really want to do that? I am always fascinated by people who say, "I'm going to try keeping the Law." That person has no idea what they are saying. That person is a carnally-minded person who is trying to please God in the flesh,. Paul makes it clear that "they that are in the flesh cannot please God" (v. 8.) Face it. It cannot be done!

We continue. Verse 9:

**9 But ye are not in the flesh, but in the Spirit, if so be that the Spirit of God dwell in you. Now if any man have not the Spirit of Christ, he is none of his.**

Works of service are fine when they are done as service to God while following "after the Spirit." Those works are not being done in the flesh since they are done while operating "in the Spirit." If anyone does not believe the gospel, then they do not have the Spirit of Christ and that person does not belong to Him. However, if they do believe the gospel, they are in the Spirit and not in the flesh as far as God is concerned. As believers, we are no longer in the flesh. We are in the Spirit. This is a *positional truth.*

The Galatian believers had lost sight of this. They were affected by outsiders who were saying that grace was not enough. This changed the truth of their salvation! As a result, they had lost their commitment to being fully spiritually-minded by adding the requirement of works to their salvation. What was Paul's response? Galatians 3:1–4:

**1 O foolish Galatians, who hath bewitched you, that ye should not obey the truth, before whose eyes Jesus**

**Christ hath been evidently set forth, crucified among you? 2 This only would I learn of you, Received ye the Spirit by the works of the law, or by the hearing of faith? 3 Are ye so foolish? having begun in the Spirit, are ye now made perfect by the flesh? 4 Have ye suffered so many things in vain? if it be yet in vain.**

The Galatians had listened to people who had come into the assembly saying that they must also follow the Mosaic Law. They began by believing the gospel alone. Although the Galatians started out being spiritually-minded, when the Jews showed up, they added *legalism* which is in the flesh. What is *legalism? Legalism* is when someone creates a requirement(s) to do or not do something in order to qualify for either receiving salvation or maintaining salvation. *Legalism* is attempting to *fulfill the Law* and, as we have seen, that is contrary to following after the Spirit. It is following after the flesh. Fulfilling works as a requirement for either obtaining or maintaining their salvation is the same as "walking after the flesh." It is striving to become righteous by works,. That, my friend, is clearly "walking after the flesh."

Let us move on. Romans 8:10–11:

**10 And if Christ be in you, the body is**

**dead because of sin; but the Spirit is life because of righteousness. 11 But if the Spirit of him that raised up Jesus from the dead dwell in you, he that raised up Christ from the dead shall also quicken your mortal bodies by his Spirit that dwelleth in you.**

Again, we are not in the flesh but in the Spirit. Those who have the Spirit are of God; those who do not are not of God. This is a *positional truth*. Paul goes on to say that the body is dead and the Spirit is life. The spirit is life because of righteousness. The same Spirit that raised Christ from the dead is making our mortal bodies alive because the Spirit dwells in us. Verses 12–14:

> **12 Therefore, brethren, we are debtors, not to the flesh, to live after the flesh. 13 For if ye live after the flesh, ye shall die: but if ye through the Spirit do mortify the deeds of the body, ye shall live. 14 For as many as are led by the Spirit of God, they are the sons of God.**

Here, Paul is talking about the absence of spiritual life being manifested. The word *manifest* means *to become clearly apparent*. Instead of manifesting the spiritual life that God has given us, we manifest death when we walk in the flesh. What does Paul mean by the words "do mortify the deeds of the body?" This means that we have to subdue it, to keep it in subjection to the will of God. We are to follow after the truth of God.

We are never going to get rid of our flesh while we remain in our earthly bodies. However, through the Spirit, we can subdue the flesh and keep it in subjection to the truth of God's Word. That is what Paul is talking about here. We know that those who are led by the Spirit of God are the sons of God. Being led by the Spirit is evidence of being a son of God. The phrase *sons of God* is generic. The word *sonship* has to do with a relationship with God. This is a position; not a gender. Therefore, those led by the Spirit of God are "the sons of God." When we believed the gospel, we were sealed by the Spirit. Now that we have the Spirit dwelling within us, Paul urges us to focus on following after the Spirit. One might ask, "How can we be spiritually-minded in Christ?"

Paul answers this question for us when we continue with Romans 8. It may surprise you. It is a lot easier than you may think.

# 14

## Romans 8 (Part II)

So far, we learned that we cannot serve God in the flesh. We can only serve God when we are led by the Spirit. The renewing of our mind is through the Word of God. Finally, we can never forget our position. Those who are led by the Spirit are the "sons of God." Romans 8:14–15:

> 14 **<u>For as many as are led by the Spirit of God, they are the sons of God</u>. 15 For ye have not received the spirit of bondage again to fear; but ye have received the Spirit of adoption, whereby we cry, Abba, Father.**

We have our *sonship* because we have been adopted into God's family. We are no longer bound to a spirit of fear, but, rather, we have received the Holy Spirit. As sons of God, we have been adopted into the household of God. We have the right to call Him *Abba*, which means Father.

Let us look at the position of *sonship* and how it is viewed differently in the Bible. First, let us go to Exodus. In the following verses, God gives instruction to Moses on what he should say to Pharaoh. Exodus 4:21–23:

> **21 And the LORD said unto Moses, When thou goest to return into Egypt, see that thou do all those wonders before Pharaoh, which I have put in thine hand: but I will harden his heart, that he shall not let the people go. 22 And thou shalt say unto Pharaoh, Thus saith the LORD, <u>Israel is my son</u>, even my firstborn: 23 And I say unto thee, <u>Let my son go, that he may serve me</u>: and if thou refuse to let him go, behold, I will slay thy son, even thy firstborn.**

Moses is instructed to show Pharaoh miracles, signs, and wonders. This was the means by which Moses was to authenticate his relationship to God as His messenger. God was sending a message through Moses. He would demand that Pharaoh let His people go. However, God would harden Pharaoh's heart and he would refuse. Let us look at the two references made with the word *son*. An ultimatum was presented along with a warning of the consequence if Pharaoh did not comply. He was to let Israel, God's firstborn son, go or else suffer the consequences. Pharaoh refused. As a result, God killed Pharaoh's firstborn son, the heir to the throne of Egypt. God called the entire nation of Israel "his firstborn son." Obviously, it was not an individual. It was a *position*.

Next, let us go to Luke 3:23:

**23 And Jesus himself began to be about thirty years of age, being (as was supposed) the son of Joseph, which was the son of Heli,**

There follows a long genealogy which traces the lineage of the Lord Jesus Christ all the way back to Adam. Verse 38:

**38 Which was the son of Enos, which was the son of Seth, which was the son of Adam, which was <u>the son of God.</u>**

Jesus' genealogy concludes with "which was the son of Adam, which was the son of God." Here, Adam is called "the son of God." Obviously, Adam is not the Lord Jesus Christ. Adam was a created being. He was made by God and given the breath of life by Him.

With these examples, we can see that the word *son* is used in different contexts within Scripture. It does not always refer to a *physical* relationship. Sometimes, as it is with our case, it is *positional*.

Since we are new creatures in Christ, we are called "the sons of God." Although we are a new creation, we are not "begotten sons." That fact becomes apparent in the Gospel of John. Many Christians recognize this passage as Jesus speaks to Nicodemus. John 3:7:

> 7 **Marvel not that I said unto thee, Ye must be born again.**

In the King James Bible, it is easy to identify the plural form of the pronoun *you* which is *ye*. Jesus is not referring to an individual as most people believe. It is the plural form of *you* and must refer to multiple people. Stop and look at the context. The phrase "ye must be born again," refers collectively to the rulers of Israel. In Exodus, God called the whole nation His firstborn son. With this in mind, it makes sense that Jesus tells Nicodemus that *the entire nation* must be born again. Collectively, Israel needed a spiritual rebirth beginning with their leaders. 1 Peter 1:3:

> 3 **Blessed be the God and Father of our Lord Jesus Christ, which according to**

**his abundant mercy hath <u>begotten us</u> <u>again</u> unto a lively hope by the resurrec- tion of Jesus Christ from the dead,**

The true believers of Israel are the true Israel. When they receive the Spirit, they will be begotten again. Jesus referred to that in John 3. Israel needs to experience a spiritual rebirth. However, those who are saved by grace are "sons of God." We were adopted the moment we believed the Gospel of Grace. We are now "a new creation in Christ." Re- member this. We are not "born again!" We are spe- cifically created by God to be "the sons of God."

Paul confirms that we are a "new creature in Christ." 2 Corinthians 5: 17:

**17 Therefore <u>if any man be in Christ, he</u> <u>is a new creature</u>: old things are passed away; behold, all things are become new.**

We are a "new creature" in Christ and adopted as sons of God. (See Romans 8:15, 23; 9:4; Galatians 4:5; Ephesians 1:5.) We were created as sons of God and not born again. The old things have passed away and all things are new. When Paul says, "all things are become new," what does he mean? First, we know that we are no longer under the Law. Second, we know that we are a new creation in Christ. How? The Body of Christ is neither Jew nor Gentile. (See Galatians 3:28.) Up to that point, a person was either a Jew or a non-Jew. This validates the fact we are something new. Why? It never existed before. This was all a mystery and hidden until the Gospel of Grace was given to Paul by the risen Lord.

Look at Galatians 4:1–5:

**1 Now I say, That the heir, as long as he is a child, differeth nothing from a servant, though he be lord of all; 2 But is under tutors and governors until the time appointed of the father. 3 Even so we, when we were children, were in bondage under the elements of the world: 4 But when the fulness of the time was come, God sent forth his Son, made of a woman, made under the law, 5 To redeem them that were under the law, that we might receive <u>the adoption of sons.</u>**

We have been legally adopted into the position of *sonship*. This takes us from being under the law to calling God *Abba Father*. The word *Abba* is similar to the names of *Daddy* and *Papa*. These are used in the intimate relationship between a father and a child.

248

Many people think of God as being a distant entity or force that is in heaven. For us, God says He is now our Father and that we are his sons because we are in Christ. It is like the connection with a physical father. It is a very special relationship.

Let us go to the Gospel of Mark. The Lord and His disciples are in the Garden of Gethsemane. This is just before the soldiers come to take Him away to be crucified. Jesus is praying to His Father. Mark 14:36:

> 36 **And he said, Abba, Father, all things are possible unto thee; take away this cup from me: nevertheless not what I will, but what thou wilt.**

Jesus used the word *Abba* when He referred to His Heavenly Father. Think about this for a moment. We can also call upon the name *Abba Father* just like Jesus did. You and I, as members of the Body of Christ, now have the same kind of relationship with the Father. We are as close to the Father as Jesus is. Stop and just let that sink in!

We return to Romans 8:14:

> 14 **For as many as are led by the Spirit of God, they are the sons of God.**

We are a *new creation* and adopted as "the sons of God." Therefore, unlike Israel, we do not need to be *born again*. Verse 15:

> 15 **For ye have not received the spirit of bondage again to fear; but ye have received the Spirit of adoption, whereby we cry, Abba, Father.**

Paul tells us that we have not received "the spirit of bondage" in which we have fear. To what is Paul referring? Let us turn to Hebrews 2:14-15:

> 14 **Forasmuch then as the children are partakers of flesh and blood, he also himself likewise took part of the same; that through death he might destroy him that had the power of death, that is, the devil; 15 And deliver them who through fear of death were all their lifetime subject to bondage.**

The writer of Hebrews is speaking of the Lord Jesus Christ and what He did for Israel. It is this to which Paul refers when he says, "we have not received the spirit of bondage again to fear." What their Messiah did for Israel was to take away the power of death from Satan. Furthermore, He delivered those who were in constant fear, throughout their lifetime, of judgment and death. They left the bondage of Egypt only to be placed under the bondage of the Law. That bondage was their striving to live up to the Law. Satan accused Israel of being unworthy. For that reason, Satan is called "the accuser of the brethren." He accuses the brethren both day and night according to Revelation 12:10. Satan accuses them of being unworthy since they cannot keep the Law. Satan has the legal right to say, "They should die. They are not worthy!" The people of Israel, in particular, were in constant fear of death because they knew that, if they did not obey the Law, there was Judgment.

Paul addresses Jews who are saved by grace. They have concerns of bondage and fear. Grace Believers have not received the spirit of bondage and fear. There is no fear of failing to live up to God's standard which is the Law of Moses. There is no fear of judgment or loss of salvation. Instead, all Grace Believers have received the spirit of adoption. All are members of God's family and, as members, He is our Father. So, we can cry *Abba Father!* Galatians 4:5:

> 5 **To redeem them that were under the law, that we might receive the adoption of sons.**

This is how the Spirit of God, through faith in the Word of God, takes us out of Adam and places us into Christ. It is what the Holy Spirit calls "the spirit of adoption." It mirrors human adoption. According to lawful aspects of adoption, we are legally members of God's family with all the rights and privileges of *sonship*. We are taken out of Adam and placed "in Christ."

Look at 1 Corinthians 12:13:

**13 For by one Spirit are we all baptized into one body, whether we be Jews or Gentiles, whether we be bond or free; and have been all made to drink into one Spirit.**

Notice that we were *all* baptized into the Body of Christ. We were all "taken out of Adam" and "placed into Christ." Who did this? The Holy Spirit calls Him "the spirit of adoption." Verses 15:21–22:

**21 For since by man came death, by man came also the resurrection of the dead. 22 For as in Adam all die, even so in Christ shall all be made alive.**

How did we go from being "in Adam" to being "in Christ?" The Holy Spirit put us there the moment we believed the gospel. The Spirit took us out of our state or position in which we were without hope.

Then, He placed us "in Christ." Now, not only do we have salvation and hope, by adoption, we also received our *sonship*.

Let us revisit Romans 8:14:

**14 For as many as are led by the Spirit of God, <u>they are the sons of God.</u>**

We will pick up our discussion concerning what it means to be "led by the Spirit." We can start by going to John 14:15–17:

**15 If ye love me, keep my commandments. 16 And I will pray the Father, and he shall give you another Comforter, that he may abide with you for ever; 17 Even the Spirit of truth; whom the world cannot receive, because it seeth him not, neither knoweth him: but ye know him; for he dwelleth with you, and shall be in you.**

The Holy Spirit is called "the Comforter." He is also "the Spirit of Truth," and "the Spirit of Adoption." This is the One and only Holy Spirit! John continues. Verse 18:

**18 I will not leave you comfortless: I will**

**come to you.**

Jesus is saying that, through the Holy Spirit, He Himself will come to them. John 16:13:

> 13 **Howbeit when he, the Spirit of truth, is come, he will guide you into all truth: for he shall not speak of himself; but whatsoever he shall hear, that shall he speak: and he will shew you things to come.**

When the Spirit of Truth comes, He will guide those to whom He is sent into all Truth. When someone is guided, what is really happening? What action is taking place? When someone is guided, they are being led or instructed.

We continue with John 16:7-11:

> 7 **Nevertheless I tell you the truth; It is expedient for you that I go away: for if I go not away, the Comforter will not come unto you; but if I depart, I will send him unto you.** 8 **And when he is come, he will reprove the world of sin, and of righteousness, and of judgment:** 9 **Of sin, because they believe not on me;** 10 **Of righteousness, because I go to my**

**Father, and ye see me no more; 11 Of judgment, because the prince of this world is judged.**

We see that the Holy Spirit will reprove the world of sin and of righteousness. Can you think of a verse in Paul's letters where it talks about being reproved? Let us compare the above to 2 Timothy 3:16–17:

**16 All scripture is given by inspiration of God, and is profitable for doctrine, for reproof, for correction, for instruction in righteousness: 17 That the man of God may be perfect, throughly furnished unto all good works.**

What is the point with these verses? I will tie this all together shortly. In Romans 8, Paul writes, "for as many as are led by the spirit of God, they are the sons of God" (v. 14). We know it is the Holy Spirit Who guides us and instructs us as the *Comforter*. With that, here is a question: "What does the Spirit of God use to lead us?"

The answer is so simple that it may surprise you. It is the Word of God! Therefore, if we are led by the Spirit of God, then we are reading the Word of God rightly divided. Because we believe, the Spirit will teach us through the Word. That is how we know we are being led by the Spirit of God. We believe what the words on the page say and then apply them to our life. It is the Spirit of God Who leads us. How does He do that? The Spirit leads us by the Word of God. Romans 8:16:

**16 The Spirit itself beareth witness with our spirit, that we are the children of God:**

Allow me to make a point here. I am not sure whether you missed this, but Paul used the word *itself* when referring to the Holy Spirit. Well, as we know, the Holy Spirit is not an "It." The Holy Spirit is the third Person of the Trinity. The word *spirit,* in the original Greek, is *neuter.* The word *neuter* means *neither masculine or feminine.* For that reason, the neuter pronouns *it* and *itself* are used when translating the original Greek. Certainly, it does not refer to the Holy Spirit as being a *thing* or an *it.* We read, "the Spirit Itself bears witness along with our spirit that we are the children of God." How does that work?

Below, we find an example of the Holy Spirit who "beareth witness with our spirit." Galatians 3:1:

**1 O foolish Galatians, who hath bewitched you, that ye should not obey**

**the truth, before whose eyes Jesus Christ hath been evidently set forth, crucified among you?**

Notice what he says here. He is asking the Galatians if they received the Spirit by the works of the Law or by the hearing of faith. We know that elsewhere, Paul instructs us that "faith cometh by hearing, and hearing by the word of God"(Rom. 10:17). So, when we heard the gospel and believed it, we received the Spirit of God. Let each of us ask ourselves this question, "How does the Holy Spirit bear witness with my spirit that I am a child of God?"

If we believe the gospel, then we believe what the Bible says. How does the Spirit lead us? The Spirit leads us by revealing to us the Word of God. Verse 3:

**3 Are ye so foolish? having begun <u>in the Spirit</u>, are ye now made perfect by the flesh?**

The Galatians had a problem. They believed the gospel at first, but then Judaizers came in. These Judaizers told them that they also needed to keep the Law in addition to believing that Christ died for their sins. They became very confused. Paul had to straighten them out. He told them they began in the Spirit. In other words, they believed the words of the gospel alone. Paul asks them if they are now made perfect through their own efforts by trying to keep the Law. It is easy to figure out how the Holy Spirit bears witness with our spirit. Our faith is in what the Word of God says and it is the Holy Spirit Who reveals it to us!

We move on. Romans 8:17:

**17 And if children, then heirs; heirs of God, and joint-heirs with Christ; if so be that we suffer with him, that we may be also glorified together.**

If we are led by the Spirit of God, then it is because we are reading the Word of God rightly divided. We do this because we believe what the Spirit is teaching us is truth. That is how we know we are both children of God and joint-heirs with Christ because we are being led by the Spirit of God. Again, how do we know that? We know that because we are reading, studying, and believing His Word.

These are wonderful promises of God. We may suffer in this world because of who we are in Christ. However, we have the assurance through His promises that we will also be glorified with Him at His Calling – the Rapture.

# 15

## Romans 8 (Part III)

If Paul's epistles were building a house, then the book of Romans would be its foundation. Everyone needs to read the Book of Romans. If they did, then they might understand God's plan for them and accept His wonderful Gospel of Grace. Paul's teachings are the doctrinal foundation for the Body of Christ – those who are saved by grace through faith without works. (See Ephesians 2:8-9.)

In the last chapter, we learned that we are children of God. And, if we are, then we are also heirs of God and joint-heirs with Christ. Therefore, we should not be surprised when we suffer with Him. At the Rapture, we will also be glorified with Him. His Spirit confirms that we are the children of God because we believed the Word of God. This applies especially to the Gospel of Grace. Paul tells us that he was given the Dispensation of the Grace of God. It was personally given to him by the resurrected Lord for the benefit of the Gentiles. Ephesians 3:2–7:

> 2 **If ye have heard of <u>the dispensation of the grace of God</u> which is given me to you-ward: 3 How that by revelation he [Christ] made known unto me the mystery; (as I wrote afore in few words, 4 Whereby, when ye read, ye may understand my knowledge in the mystery of Christ) 5 Which in other ages was not made known unto the sons of men, as it is now revealed unto his holy apostles and prophets by the Spirit;**
>
> 6 **That the Gentiles should be fellow-heirs, and of the same body, and partakers of his promise in Christ by the gospel: 7 Whereof <u>I was made a minister, according to the gift of the grace of God given unto me</u> by the effectual working of his power.**

Some people interpret verse 6 incorrectly. They say that those saved by grace are fellow heirs "with Israel." However, that is not at all what the verse says. We are fellow heirs "with Christ" and "of the same Body." He is speaking about the Body of Christ. When we believed the gospel, the Spirit of

God spiritually placed us in the Body of Christ. This makes us partakers of His promise as fellow heirs. What promise is this? It is the promise of the Gospel of Grace which Paul received from Christ.

As joint heirs with Christ, we will receive a portion of His inheritance with Him. We will rule and reign with Christ in the heavenly places. Although Christ will inherit everything, as it pertains to the Body of Christ, our inheritance relates solely to heavenly places. Paul teaches that God has "blessed us with all spiritual blessings in heavenly places in Christ" (Eph. 1:3). That is where our inheritance is. We read at the beginning of the Bible, "God created the heaven and the earth" (Gen. 1:1). The Body of Christ will inherit *heavenly places* while Israel will inherit *earthly places* – both of which accomplished by gracious acts of God.

There is a controversy among Christians concerning the following verse. Romans 8:17:

> 17 **And if children, then heirs; heirs of God, and joint-heirs with Christ; if so be that we suffer with him, that we may be also glorified together.**

They have a problem with the last portion of the verse, "if so be that we suffer with him, that we may be also glorified together." They teach that unless we suffer, we are not going to be glorified. When they teach about suffering, they equate suffering with being persecuted for the faith. They make our inheritance and glorification contingent upon our suffering persecution. Many of these teachers also teach that the Body of Christ will go through the Tribulation as well. There is a big problem with that. We know from Paul's teaching that every single believer will be glorified regardless of whether they are persecuted or not. Our inheritance and our glorification are promised to all believers. They are guaranteed!

Let us go to Ephesians 1: 12–14:

**12 That we should be to the praise of his glory, who first trusted in Christ. 13 In whom ye also trusted, after that ye heard the word of truth, the gospel of your salvation: in whom also after that ye believed, ye were sealed with that holy Spirit of promise, 14 Which is the earnest of our inheritance until the redemption of the purchased possession, unto the praise of his glory.**

The "praise of his glory" is a reference to the Rapture. So, those who believe the gospel have a promised inheritance and are sealed unto the Day of Redemption. That day, we will all be like Christ; we will all be glorified.

Let us look at Philippians 3:20–21:

**20 For our conversation is in heaven; from whence also we look for the Saviour, the Lord Jesus Christ: 21 Who shall change our vile body, that it may be fashioned like unto his glorious body, according to the working whereby he is able even to subdue all things unto himself.**

Our *conversation* is who we are. It is our identity; our lifestyle. Therefore, our *conversation* is in heaven because our identity is *in Christ*. It is toward heaven that we look with hope for our Savior. He shall change our earthly bodies into one similar to His own glorified body. That is the promise made to every believer. Every believer will be raptured, receive their glorified body, and receive their inheritance in Christ.

If we are heirs of God and joint heirs with Christ, then we will also suffer with Him. This is a given. Let us understand what Paul means by this. 1 Corinthians 4:11–13:

11 Even unto this present hour we both hunger, and thirst, and are naked, and are buffeted, and have no certain dwelling place; 12 And labour, working with our own hands: being reviled, we bless; being persecuted, we suffer it: 13 Being defamed, we intreat: we are made as the filth of the world, and are the offscouring of all things unto this day.

Let us also look at 1 Corinthians 6:7:

7 Now therefore there is utterly a fault among you, because ye go to law one with another. Why do ye not rather take wrong? why do ye not rather suffer yourselves to be defrauded?

There are different kinds of suffering that the believer will go through. It may be persecution for the faith, but there are other ways we can suffer as well. All of this is because of the Enemy. 1 Corinthians 9:12:

12 If others be partakers of this power over you, are not we rather? Nevertheless we have not used this power; but suffer all things, lest we should hinder the gospel of Christ.

There are sacrifices that we will make, but we are not to hinder the gospel of Christ. Now, go to 1 Corinthians 12:26:

> 26 **And whether one member suffer, all the members suffer with it; or one member be honoured, all the members rejoice with it.**

If one member of the local assembly suffers, then all the members suffer. However, if one member is honored or has good news, then all the members rejoice. This is an example of the kind of suffering which we share as the Body of Christ. Another pertinent reference is found in Philippians 1:29:

> 29 **For unto you it is given in the behalf of Christ, not only to believe on him, but also to suffer for his sake;**

It is a given fact that, in some form or fashion, we will suffer as a believer. These verses present some ways in which we could suffer from external sources. There is another way we most definitely suffer. We all suffer as a result of being at war constantly with our old man which is our sin nature. We are constantly fighting a battle to keep that old man of sin in check, to keep our flesh in check, and to keep it in submission to the new man. That is also a form of suffering.

We move on. Romans 8:18:

**18 For I reckon that the sufferings of this present time are not worthy to be compared with the glory which shall be revealed in us.**

Paul makes an important statement here. Everyone in the Body of Christ suffers. We also have a promise which is guaranteed. Someday we will be glorified. We will meet the Lord in the air at His Calling – the Rapture. He will give us our glorified body. From that point on, we will be forever with the Lord. That is our hope of glory!

We continue. Verse 19:

**19 For the earnest expectation of the creature waiteth for the manifestation of the sons of God.**

The word *manifestation* means *the act of revealing something once unseen but now visible.* We wait in earnest expectation for the time when the corruption we are presently experiencing, will be turned to incorruption. That, my friends, is the *manifestation* of the sons of God. One day it will be revealed that we are the sons of God because we will have our glorified bodies like that of Christ. (See Philippians 3.)

Let us look at another reference. 2 Corinthians 4:16–18:

> 16 **For which cause we faint not; but though our outward man perish, yet the inward man is renewed day by day.** 17 **For our light affliction, which is but for a moment, worketh for us a far more exceeding and eternal weight of glory;** 18 **While we look not at the things which are seen, but at the things which are not seen: for the things which are seen are temporal; but the things which are not seen are eternal.**

The body that perishes is the body in which we now live. When we compare these two verses, we see they are almost identical. Let us repeat Romans 8:18–19:

> 18 **For I reckon that <u>the sufferings of this present time</u> are not worthy to be compared with <u>the glory which shall be revealed in us.</u>** 19 **For the earnest expectation of the creature waiteth for <u>the manifestation of the sons of God.</u>**

Now we can understand what Paul means by "the earnest expectation of the creature waits for the manifestation of the sons of God" (v. 19). We all wait for the day when we will be raptured and receive the fulfillment of the promise. When we receive our glorified bodies, our redemption will be complete.

On earth we are going to suffer and experience what Paul calls *light affliction,* but it is only for a moment. How can Paul call it light affliction? How can he say it is just for a moment? Well, in the future we will look back and see it as God sees it now. When compared to eternity, it was momentarily just light affliction. Yet, it has a purpose. This temporary suffering or affliction presently works for our benefit. When we look at it from God's eternal perspective, it works for us exceedingly and abundantly towards our glory. At present, we see only the temporal things; not the eternal. Let us get an idea of what is planned for us. 2 Corinthians 5:1:

> 1 **For we know that if our earthly house of this tabernacle were dissolved, we have a building of God, an house not made with hands, eternal in the heavens.**

The word *tabernacle* means *dwelling.* It refers to our physical bodies which will someday return to dust. However, we are promised a dwelling-place not made with human hands. It will be eternal in the heavens. Friend, there is no mansion on a hilltop for us. Each believer is getting a new body! Verse 2:

> 2 **For in this we groan, earnestly desiring to be clothed upon with our house which is from heaven:**

Do you remember the word *groan* mentioned earlier? We are going to see that word *groan* show up again. We will understand exactly the point Paul is making. We are *groaning* because we long for the day when all of our physical problems will go away and we will receive our glorified body. Let us jump down to verse 4:

> 4 **For we that are in this tabernacle do groan, being burdened: not for that we would be unclothed, but clothed upon, that mortality might be swallowed up of life.**

In our present bodies, we *groan*. God will not leave us naked. He has prepared for us an immortal body in which we will be clothed for an eternity with Him. Here is a comparable reference. 1 Corinthians 15: 54:

**54** So when this corruptible shall have put on incorruption, and this mortal shall have put on immortality, then shall be brought to pass the saying that is written, Death is swallowed up in victory.

Look at these two verses! One uses "swallowed up of [by] life." The other uses "swallowed up in victory." 2 Corinthians 5:5–8:

**5** Now he that hath wrought us for the selfsame thing is God, who also hath given unto us the earnest of the Spirit. **6** Therefore we are always confident, knowing that, whilst we are at home in the body, we are absent from the Lord: **7** (For we walk by faith, not by sight:) **8** We are confident, I say, and willing rather to be absent from the body, and to be present with the Lord.

God has made for us an eternal tabernacle or dwelling place in Christ. The word *earnest* is a legal word going back to Rome. *Earnest* means *the deposit made to guarantee the completion of a promised transaction that will occur in the future.* The Spirit is our security, our guarantee, or our *earnest.* We can be confident that God will complete His promise. When we are absent from this present body, we will be present with the Lord in our glorified bodies.

Let us go to Romans 8:20–21:

**20 For the creature was made subject to vanity, not willingly, but by reason of him who hath subjected the same in hope, 21 Because the creature itself also shall be delivered from the bondage of corruption into the glorious liberty of the children of God.**

The first human was Adam. He chose to disobey God and that resulted in the curse. He and the generations that followed after him were corrupt. Everything in creation became corrupt when the curse was put upon the earth. *Vanity* was the consequence of sin. Yet, God had planned all along to deliver Creation from the corruption of this *vanity*. God also provided the means for our deliverance. Through the Gospel of Grace, we are taken from this corruption into glorious liberty as the children of God.

We continue. Verses 22–23:

**22 For we know that the whole creation groaneth and travaileth in pain together until now. 23 And not only they, but**

**ourselves also, which have the firstfruits of the Spirit, even we ourselves groan within ourselves, waiting for the adoption, to wit, the redemption of our body.**

There is that word *groan* again. This time Paul uses the word for "the whole of creation." The word *travail* means *work especially when it is arduous or involves painful effort; to toil; to struggle as a woman in childbirth.* What does Paul mean by "the firstfruits of the Spirit?" Ephesians 1:5:

**5 Having predestinated us unto <u>the adoption of children</u> by Jesus Christ to himself, according to the good pleasure of his will,**

What was predestinated? It was the completion of the adoption of the children who trust in Christ's death, burial, and resurrection. The adoption will be completed in two phases. First, the moment we believed, we were immediately adopted into the family of God and spiritually placed "in Christ." The second phase is His Calling. This is the Rapture. It is this second phase of the adoption to which Paul refers in verse 5 above. God predestinated us to "the completion of our adoption." The word *predestinated* means *to have been predetermined or foreordained; to have determined beforehand an unchangeable purpose or series of events.* It was predetermined or foreordained, in advance, that our adoption would be completed. Why? Because God foreordained it.

There is a belief which is prevalent among believers today. It is completely different from what we discussed above. Calvinism has their own beliefs about *predestination.* They teach that God determined, in advance, those who will be saved and those will be damned for eternity. This interpretation rules out the free will of man. It is contrary to what Paul teaches, "For this is good and acceptable in the sight of God our Saviour; Who will have all men to be saved, and to come unto the know-ledge of the truth" (1 Tim. 2:3-4).

We move on. Romans 8:23:

23 **And not only they, but ourselves also, which have the firstfruits of the Spirit, even we ourselves groan within ourselves, <u>waiting for the adoption</u>, to wit, [that is to say] the redemption of our body.**

We were redeemed spiritually the moment we believed the gospel. That phase is finished. Next, we are going to be redeemed physically in the future and that will complete our adoption. Again, this physical redemption of the body will occur at the Rapture. We are going to be delivered from this present evil world and brought into heaven, our eternal home. It is at that point that we will receive our glorified body. Philippians 1:6:

**6 Being confident of this very thing, that he which hath begun a good work in you will perform it until the day of Jesus Christ:**

Christ completed all the work necessary for our salvation. It is freely offered to all but effective for only those who "choose to believe."

Let us continue. Romans 8:24:

**24 For we are saved by hope: but hope that is seen is not hope: for what a man seeth, why doth he yet hope for?**

Our hope comes from our faith in the Word of God. We are saved by the work of the Cross. The hope we have is in the unseen. We wait for His Calling which is the Rapture. It is called our *"hope of glory!"* Paul teaches about this *hope.* 1 Thessalonians 4:13:

**13 But I would not have you to be igno-**

rant, brethren, concerning them which are asleep, that ye sorrow not, even as others which have no hope.

Those who do not believe the gospel have no *hope*. Specifically, they do not have any *hope* of the Rapture and the departure before the Great Tribulation. They do not have any *hope* of a glorified body. Most importantly, they do not have any *hope* of salvation. It is this *hope* to which Paul is referring in Romans 8. Our faith is based upon His promise that we will be delivered from our present bodies. Today, it is this *hope* that saves us from sorrow, despair, and corruption. Romans 8:25:

25 But if we hope for that we see not, then do <u>we with patience wait for it</u>.

Patience is one of the byproducts of continuing to have this *hope*. Our *hope* is that one day all our problems will be gone. On that day, we are going to be delivered from all the problems and suffering we are experiencing in this present life. We have this wonderful promise from God and that gives us hope. We have hope because we believe in what God says. This is the hope about which Paul is teaching.

Every student of the Bible must study the Scriptures for themselves. We are to be persuaded in our own mind by the Scriptures what verses in the Bible mean. Commentaries by seasoned believers are highly beneficial, but they are not equal to the authority of Scripture. Anything beyond the Word of God, whether written in books or spoken from the pulpit, is commentary. We need to be like the more noble Bereans who "received the word with all readiness of mind, and searched the scriptures daily, [to see] whether those things were so" (Acts 17:11). Therefore, let every student of the Bible be fully persuaded in their own mind.

We move on. Verse 26:

**26 Likewise the Spirit also helpeth our infirmities: for we know not what we should pray for as we ought: but the Spirit itself maketh intercession for us with groanings which cannot be uttered.**

Paul begins this verse with *"likewise."* We could use the words "similar to the above." Paul says, "the spirit itself beareth witness with our spirit that we are the children of God" (v. 16). He later writes "the Spirit itself makes intercession for us with groanings which cannot be uttered" (v. 26). So, the Spirit bears witness concerning our *sonship* and also helps us with our *infirmities*. The word *infirmity* means *a con-*

*dition of being infirm, often as associated with old age; weakness, frailty; a bodily ailment.*

This *hope* of our bodily redemption gives us patience and peace. The Spirit helps us not to sorrow like others who have no hope. The infirmities we suffer are part of being in our physical body of flesh. We suffer because we remain in this mortal body on earth. Paul says, "likewise the Spirit also helps us with our infirmities." Sometimes, we do not know what to pray. That is a very curious statement. Why would Paul say this? Paul gives us instructions and models on how to pray throughout his letters. However, think about this. Does Paul, in any of his letters, give us specific instructions on how to pray about infirmities?

The closest we can get to that would be in Philippians 4:6–7:

> **6 Be careful for nothing; but in every thing by prayer and supplication with thanksgiving let your requests be made known unto God. 7 And the peace of God, which passeth all understanding, shall keep your hearts and minds through Christ Jesus.**

The above was the only place I found in Paul's letters

that instructs believers  about prayer for our concerns; especially our infirmities.

Paul makes a reference to his own personal prayers concerning an infirmity – "a thorn in the flesh." 2 Corinthians 12:7–10:

> 7 **And lest I should be exalted above measure through the abundance of the revelations, there was given to me a thorn in the flesh, the messenger of Satan to buffet me, lest I should be exalted above measure.** 8 **For this thing I besought the Lord thrice, that it might depart from me.**
>
> 9 **And he said unto me, My grace is sufficient for thee: for my strength is made perfect in weakness. Most gladly therefore will I rather glory in my infirmities, that the power of Christ may rest upon me.** 10 **Therefore I take pleasure in infirmities, in reproaches, in ne- cessities, in persecutions, in distresses for Christ's sake: for when I am weak, then am I strong.**

There are lot of believers who think this is a model on how to pray about our infirmities. Wait a minute. Paul wrote that we know not how we should pray. We know from Paul's letters how to pray for the lost, how to pray for greater spiritual understanding, and how to pray for spiritual maturity. Yet, in 2 Corinthians 12, Paul asked the Lord three times to remove "a thorn in the flesh." The Lord's response revealed something to him. God responded to Paul's request with, "My grace is sufficient for thee" (v. 9). Note that Paul used the word *thee* which is the singular form of the pronoun *you*. Will this be God's answer to every prayer when we pray about our infirmities? Absolutely not! Although that is what a lot of people think it means. When we pray and ask God, we know that His answer may be yes, no, or not at this time. However, in Paul's case, he learned that God's strength is made perfect in his weakness. For the rest of us, when we do not know what to pray, the Spirit will do it for us!

Here is a situation involving the health of Paul's companion. Philippians 2:25–28:

> 25 Yet I supposed it necessary to send to you Epaphroditus, my brother, and companion in labour, and fellow-soldier, but your messenger, and he that ministered to my wants. 26 For he longed after you all, and was full of heaviness, because that ye had heard

that he had been sick. 27 For indeed he was sick nigh unto death: but God had mercy on him; and not on him only, but on me also, lest I should have sorrow upon sorrow. 28 I sent him therefore the more carefully, that, when ye see him again, ye may rejoice, and that I may be the less sorrowful.

God had mercy on Epaphroditus who was sick even to the point of death. There seems to be no formula for praying for infirmities. Sometimes there is healing; sometimes there is not. The book of Job provides a study on the question as to why that is.

The Spirit knew Paul's need when he appeared in court for the charges brought against him. 2 Timothy 4:16–18:

16 At my first answer no man stood with me, but all men forsook me: I pray God that it may not be laid to their charge. 17 Notwithstanding the Lord stood with me, and strengthened me; that by me the preaching might be fully known, and that all the Gentiles might hear: and I was delivered out of the mouth of the lion. 18 And the Lord shall deliver me from every evil work, and will pre-

**serve me unto his heavenly kingdom: to whom be glory for ever and ever. Amen.**

The Lord stood with Paul and strengthened him. In his moment of need, God comforted him.

The Lord does not always heal. Verse 20:

**20 Erastus abode at Corinth: but Trophimus have I left at Miletum sick.**

Paul had to leave one of his fellow laborers behind because he was sick. We have no established pattern for prayer when it comes to physical healing. Sometimes people are delivered from physical illness. In Paul's case, God said no, but reminded him that His grace is sufficient. Paul writes that we know not how to pray about infirmities. Our consolation is that the Spirit intercedes for us, and speaks to God on our behalf. We must trust God for the outcome for His ways are higher than our ways, and we must have faith that whatever God chooses for us is best.

How does the Spirit make intercession for us? The Word of God is the medium by which the Spirit operates today. It is through the Word of God that the Spirit intercedes. Through the Word of God, we learn patience and receive hope. We also have the peace of God that passes all understanding when we take all of our burdens to Him. Furthermore, the Word of God gives us direction and guidance. It can give us encouragement in any situation or circumstance. Additionally, I believe the Spirit is interceding for us in another way.

Let us continue. Romans 8:27:

**27 And he that searcheth the hearts knoweth what is the mind of the Spirit, because he maketh intercession for the saints according to the will of God.**

The Spirit knows our hearts and also the will of God. Therefore, He can make intercession for us according to the will of God. We do not know what God's will is concerning our infirmities or the infirmities of others, but the Spirit knows the will of God concerning it.

Notice the word *groanings*. Where have we heard that word before? We are *groaning* within ourselves as we wait to receive our glorified bodies. Paul tells us that "the spirit itself makes intercession for us with groaning"(v. 26). These groans are coming from within us. It stems from our desire to be set free from the bondage of corruption and our infirmities. Our inner self groans for that day. We read that, "we ourselves groan within ourselves, waiting for the adoption, to wit, the redemption of our body" (v. 23). Notice that the Spirit intercedes with groanings within us "with words that cannot be uttered." Before I came to the knowledge of rightly dividing the Word of Truth, I was involved in the Pentecostal or Charismatic Movement. They would use verse 26 to support praying in tongues by saying that it was the Spirit's groanings. However, the verse is specific. It states that these groanings "cannot be uttered." This verse has nothing to do with speaking or praying in tongues. The words "cannot be uttered" simply mean that they cannot be spoken.

I will end this chapter with a brief summary of what we have learned so far. As believers saved by grace through faith, we are "in Christ!" Our salvation was paid for by His blood and sealed by the Holy Spirit until the day of redemption – the Rapture. All this happened the moment we were saved. We were ". . . sealed with that holy Spirit of promise, Which is the earnest of our inheritance until the redemption of the purchased possession, unto the praise of his glory" (Eph. 1:13-14). Stop for a moment and think about this. That is us! As believers saved by grace through faith according to Paul's gospel, we have hope that others do not have. We have the "hope of glory" which is the Rapture. In spite of what we are going through today, we have the "hope of glory."

We will receive our glorious bodies which "completes the promise of our redemption." Thereafter, we will spend eternity with Jesus Christ, our Lord and Savior.

I hope you are enjoying our journey through Paul's letter to the believers in Rome. In the next chapter, we will finish our study of Romans 8.

# 16

## Romans 8 (Part IV)

We continue our study beginning with Romans 8:28:

> **28 And we know that all things work together for good to them that love God, to them who are the called according to his purpose.**

There are different ways this verse has been interpreted. I believe that the words *all things* refer to the things we have learned so far in Romans 8. These are not *things* that we need to guess or *things* we somehow have to figure out on our own. They are *things* "that work together for our good." In this chapter, we will find that these *things* are outlined.

Look back at verse 22:

**22 For we know that the whole creation groaneth and travaileth in pain together until now.**

Paul tells us that *all* creation groans and struggles in pain together until now. Why does he say, "until now?" It is because God oversees everything and He makes sure that "all things work together for good." For whom? He does this for "them that love God, to them who are the called according to his purpose." God is sovereign over all. This applies to those who are saved by grace through faith. We have joy for the "hope of glory" to come. Also, we have the assurance that "all things work together for good." Why? It is because we are "the called" according to His purpose.

Look again at verses 24–25:

**24 For we are saved by hope: but hope that is seen is not hope: for what a man seeth, why doth he yet hope for? 25 But if we hope for that we see not, then do we with patience wait for it.**

We are "saved by hope" from our present trials and tribulations. Our *hope* is for the final stage of our redemption. This is the Rapture where we are removed from this present evil world and we receive our glorified bodies. We are saved from sorrow and despair because we have *hope*. 1 Thessalonians 4:13:

> 13 **But I would not have you to be ignorant, brethren, concerning them which are asleep, that ye sorrow not, even as others which have no hope.**

In Romans 8, Paul says we are "saved by hope." We do not despair. With that hope, we wait both patiently and assuredly for His Calling which is the Rapture. By having this hope, it works together for our good.

With that, we are now ready to move on. Verses 28–29:

> 28 **And we know that all things work together for good to them that love God, to them who are the called according to his purpose.** 29 **For whom he did foreknow, he also did predestinate to be conformed to the image of his Son, that he might be the firstborn among many brethren.**

Paul is saying that those whom God foreknew, He also predestined to be made into the image of His Son. This is another reference to the Rapture. Christ is the *firstborn* among many. Who are the many? They are ones who are saved by grace through faith. My friends, he is talking about us! Everything is working together for our good. One might ask, "How is everything working together for our good?" By knowing these things, it encourages us spiritually in our present situation. We can focus less on our present state and more on our future state.

God has predestined us "to be conformed to the image of His Son" at the Rapture. This should encourage and comfort us. It edifies us spiritually in the face of all our conflicts, trials, and tribulations. This world is crazy. In all the chaos, we have *hope* for our future. Our hope is "in Christ!" Verse 30:

> 30 **Moreover whom he did predestinate, them he also called: and whom he called, them he also justified: and whom he justified, them he also glorified.**

I really like this passage because Paul is speaking as though we are already glorified. We know that the glorification of our body is a future event, simultaneous with the Rapture. However, in God's eyes, He sees it as already done. It is a done deal. We will be glorified because we are predestined to it.

In Ephesians, Paul talks about us already being seated in the heavenly places with Christ. God "hath raised us up together, and made us sit together in heavenly places in Christ Jesus" (Eph. 2:6). As far as God is concerned, we are already there. It is a done deal. We have *hope* knowing these things are working together for our good. Verses 31–32:

> 31 **What shall we then say to these things? If God be for us, who can be against us? 32 He that spared not his own Son, but delivered him up for us all, how shall he not with him also freely give us all things?**

Paul asks, "What shall we then say to these things?" What are *these things?* They are the things that are working together for our good. He asks another question. "If God be for us, who can be against us?" As we think about these questions, someone might say, "Wait a minute. I experience all sorts of opposition!" Well, we all do.

Throughout our daily life, we all have some sort of opposition. However, the opposition about which Paul is talking is spiritual opposition from the enemy. Ephesians 6:12:

12 **For we wrestle not against flesh and**

blood, but against principalities, against powers, against the rulers of the darkness of this world, against spiritual wickedness in high places.

We find an explanation in Ephesians 1:3–8:

3 Blessed be the God and Father of our Lord Jesus Christ, who hath blessed us with all spiritual blessings in heavenly places in Christ: 4 According as he hath chosen us in him before the foundation of the world, that we should be holy and without blame before him in love: 5 Having predestinated us unto the adoption of children by Jesus Christ to himself, according to the good pleasure of his will, 6 To the praise of the glory of his grace, wherein he hath made us accepted in the beloved. 7 In whom we have redemption through his blood, the forgive-ness of sins, according to the riches of his grace; 8 Wherein he hath abounded toward us in all wisdom and prudence;

In these verses, we see *high places* and *heavenly places.* Satan and his fallen angels have not yet been cast out of heaven. Although the last quotation was rather long, it would be difficult to shorten it since the entire Scripture is consistent with what we are reading in Romans 8.

It is difficult not to be overwhelmed with gratitude when we realize that we have so many blessings from God. All of these He has freely given to us. He has blessed us with all spiritual blessings in heavenly places. Colossians 2:10:

**10 And ye are complete in him, which is the head of all principality and power:**

Yes, we are complete in Christ. We are justified and sealed to the Day of Redemption. We have Christ's righteousness imputed to us. We have all those things as present possession because we believed the gospel by faith. It includes everything that Christ has done and all that He promises to do for us in the future. We freely receive *all* these blessings when we believe the Gospel of Grace.

Let us move on. Romans 8:32:

**32 He that spared not his own Son, but delivered him up for us all, <u>how shall he not with him also freely give us all things?</u>**

Notice the words "with Him." How shall God Who gave us His Son not also freely give us all things? Paul chooses the future tense when he writes the verse. When Paul refers to *Him,* to Whom is he referring? The *Him* is Jesus Christ, God's own Son. Think of the sacrifice God made for us. Paul writes, "He spared not His own Son, but delivered Him up for us all." We will receive much more than our salvation. One might ask, "What else do we receive?"

Let us look back to the beginning of Romans 8. We see our inheritance is mentioned. Verses 16–17:

> **16 The Spirit itself beareth witness with our spirit, that we are the children of God: 17 And if children, then heirs; heirs of God, and joint-heirs with Christ; if so be that we suffer with him, that we may be also glorified together.**

This is great news! We have an inheritance. It says we are "joint-heirs with Christ." Did you catch that? He said *joint-heirs!* Everything that Christ is going to inherit in the future, we have a share in it. Why? It is because we are *joint-heirs* with Him. God has freely given us a portion of all things "in Christ!"

Concerning this inheritance, we need to rightly divide the Word of Truth. There is a division here, and I want to make sure we see it. Christ inherits everything in both heaven and earth. Indeed, He does. However, the Body of Christ does not inherit the *earthly things*. Instead, the Body of Christ inherits the *heavenly things*. Psalm 37:7–9:

> 7 **Rest in the LORD, and wait patiently for him: fret not thyself because of him who prospereth in his way, because of the man who bringeth wicked devices to pass. 8 Cease from anger, and forsake wrath: fret not thyself in any wise [way] to do evil. 9 For evildoers shall be cut off: but those that wait upon the LORD, <u>they shall inherit the earth</u>.**

King David wrote this psalm to Israel. He used words like *wait* patiently, *cease* from anger, *forsake* wrath, and *fret not*. He tells them to "wait upon the Lord." Notice the end of verse 9. David used the future tense by writing *shall*. We see that the Jews who wait upon the Lord "shall inherit the earth."

In the Sermon on the Mount, Jesus teach-es the Jews the Beatitudes. Matthew 5:1–5:

> 1 **And seeing the multitudes, he went up into a mountain: and when he was set, his disciples came unto him: 2 And he**

> opened his mouth, and taught them,
> saying, 3 Blessed are the poor in spirit:
> for theirs is the kingdom of heaven. 4
> Blessed are they that mourn: for they
> shall be comfort- ed. 5 Blessed are the
> meek: for <u>they shall inherit the earth.</u>

To whom is Christ teaching? Dispensationally, we know that He is teaching the lost house of Israel. Therefore, we see that it is believing Israel who is promised they will inherit the earth. They will be joint-heirs with Christ and their inheritance is "earthly based." However, members of the Body of Christ are also joint-heirs with our Lord, but our inheritance is "heavenly based."

Let us see how this all comes together in the end. Ephesians 1:10:

> 10 That in the dispensation of the ful-
> ness of times he might gather together
> in one all things in Christ, both <u>which
> are in heaven</u>, and <u>which are on earth;</u>
> even in him:

Christ is going to inherit everything, thereby He is gathering together all things unto Himself. This includes that "which are in heaven" and that "which are on the earth." Our part is heavenly. We are joint heirs with Christ in the heavenly portion. Colossians 1:12–13:

**12 Giving thanks unto the Father, which hath made us meet to be partakers of the inheritance of the saints in light: 13 Who hath delivered us from the power of darkness, and hath translated us into the kingdom of his dear Son:**

Now, this is referring to a spiritual kingdom and not a physical kingdom. Yes, it is the Kingdom of Christ. However, right now, it is only spiritual. We remain on earth awaiting the Rapture. Our inheritance is in the heavenlies, and it is in the future. The kingdom promised to Israel is not yet on the earth. These inheritances are guaranteed by the Word of God. The Apostle John wrote, "He that overcometh shall inherit all things; and I will be his God, and he shall be my son" (Rev. 21:7).

Continue with Colossians. Verse 18–20:

**18 And he is the head of the body, the church: who is the beginning, the firstborn from the dead; that in all things he might have the preeminence. 19 For it pleased the Father that in him should all fulness dwell; 20 And, having**

made peace through the blood of his cross, by him to reconcile all things unto himself; by him, I say, <u>whether they be things in earth, or things in heaven.</u>

Paul is speaking about Christ and pressing the point that Christ will inherit everything. As we have seen, that includes both heaven and earth. We will share in Christ's heavenly inheritance while Israel will share in His earthly inheritance.

Some Christian movements teach that, today, Christ is currently ruling from heaven. They teach that He is presently acting as King and He is in complete control of everything on earth. That is simply not true. Hebrews 2:8:

8 Thou hast put all things in subjection under his feet. For in that he put all in subjection under him, he left nothing that is not put under him. <u>But now we see not yet all things put under him.</u>

The author, writing to the Kingdom Believers, says, "But now, we see not yet all things put under him." Look at what King David wrote. Psalm 110:1:

1 The LORD said unto my Lord, Sit thou

at my right hand, until I make thine enemies thy footstool.

King David wrote what the LORD, Elohim, told David's Lord, Adonai, to wait beside Him until He subdues His enemies. Presently, Christ is seated at the right hand of God the Father. It is true that Christ is above all principalities and powers in heavenly places. However, God has not yet finished subduing His enemies. The earth is currently under the control of someone else. Ephesians 2:2:

> 2 Wherein in time past ye walked according to the course of this world, according to <u>the prince of the power of the air</u>, the spirit that now worketh in the children of disobedience:

Now, let us read again Romans 8:32–33:

> 32 He that spared not his own Son, but delivered him up for us all, how shall he not with him also freely give us all things? 33 Who shall lay any thing to the charge of God's elect? It is God that justifieth.

We all experience opposition in this world. Paul asks, "Who shall lay anything to the charge of God's elect?" Well, who would bring charges against them? Do we know who would do such a thing?

For the answer, let us look at 1 Corinthians 1:18–20:

> 18 For the preaching of the cross is to them that perish foolishness; but unto us which are saved it is the power of God. 19 For it is written, I will destroy the wisdom of the wise, and will bring to nothing the understanding of the prudent. 20 Where is the wise? where is the scribe? where is the disputer of this world? hath not God made foolish the wisdom of this world?

Who is the disputer of this world? Who is accusing the brethren? I think we know the answer, but let us see it in God's Word. Revelation 12:10:

> 10 And I heard a loud voice saying in heaven, Now is come salvation, and strength, and the kingdom of our God, and the power of his Christ: <u>for the accuser of our brethren is cast down, which accused them before our God day and night</u>.

Satan is the accuser of the brethren. He is the disputer of this world.

Notice below that Paul calls Satan "the god of this world." 2 Corinthians 4:4:

> **4 In whom <u>the god of this world</u> hath blinded the minds of them which believe not, lest the light of the glorious gospel of Christ, who is the image of God, should shine unto them.**

Satan had been granted authority over the world until Adam was given dominion over it. When Adam sinned, Satan claimed that dominion. Christ did not dispute that during His temptations in the wilderness. (See Matthew 4:1-11.) Satan's third and final temptation, or testing, is shared in Matthew 4:8–10:

> **8 Again, the devil taketh him up into an exceeding high mountain, and sheweth him all the kingdoms of the world, and the glory of them; 9 And saith unto him, All these things will I give thee, if thou wilt fall down and worship me. 10 Then saith Jesus unto him, Get thee hence, Satan: for it is written, Thou shalt worship the Lord thy God, and him only shalt thou serve.**

Instead of disputing Satan's claim, Jesus responded to him with Scripture. The Word of God is sharper than any two-edged sword. Paul asked, "Who shall lay anything to the charge of God's elect?" (v. 33).We now know about whom he is talking. Satan may be the one that accuses, but God has already justified us, redeemed us, paid for our sins, and pronounced us righteous in Christ.

We continue. Romans 8:34:

**34 Who is he that condemneth? It is Christ that died, yea rather, that is risen again, who is even at the right hand of God, who also maketh intercession for us.**

The Holy Spirit intercedes for us when we do not know what to pray. The Lord Jesus Christ also intercedes for us with God the Father. Think about that. We have two members of the Trinity interceding for us at all times. How comforting is that! They do this so that "all things work together for good to them that love God, to them who are the called according to his purpose" (Rom. 8:28). Paul discusses in Romans 8 the things that are "working together for our good."

We can be confident in God's love for us. Paul

lists everything that cannot separate us from His love. Verse 35:

**35 Who shall separate us from the love of Christ? shall tribulation, or distress, or persecution, or famine, or nakedness, or peril, or sword?**

Why would some Christians think that anything would separate them from the love of Christ? It has to do with them believing that they are Israel. Under the Law of Moses, Israel was in right-standing when they kept His commandments. When they did, He blessed them. When they did not, He cursed them. (See Deuteronomy 30:15–20.) Today, many Christians believe they are Israel. How is this possible?

They bring the Mosaic Law into the Dispensation of Grace. This happens because a *blenderized* theology is taught in churches today. Sadly, most Christians believe that if things are not going well, God must be mad at them. Somehow, God has forsaken them otherwise this would not be happening to them. Does that sound familiar? It is for that reason Paul addresses this issue in Romans 8. Here, he makes it clear that nothing can separate us from the love of Christ. Nothing! If bad things happen to us, it has absolutely nothing whatsoever to do with our standing with the Lord. I would like to remind you of the *hope* we have by repeating verse 8:18:

> 18 **For I reckon that the sufferings of this present time are not worthy to be compared with the glory which shall be revealed in us.**

We move on. Romans 8:36:

> 36 **As it is written, For thy sake we are killed all the day long; we are accounted as sheep for the slaughter.**

The above is a quote from Psalm 44:22–24:

> 22 **Yea, for thy sake are we killed all the day long; we are counted as sheep for the slaughter. 23 Awake, why sleepest thou, O Lord? arise, cast us not off for ever. 24 Wherefore hidest thou thy face, and forgettest our affliction and our oppression?**

King David wrote to the Jews. When things go badly and God does not fix it right away, some believers were perplexed and despaired. They might have asked, "Why doesn't God help us?" Paul included this psalm for a reason. We find the reason in Romans 8:37:

**37 Nay, in all these things we are more than conquerors through him that loved us.**

Paul uses this psalm as an example of what some people might say when they are in difficult situations. We must see past the present and see our future. Paul answers, "Nay, in all these things we are more than conquerors through Him that loved us." Whether we are heavily persecuted, thrown in jail because of our faith, without food, or unable to pay our rent, Paul tells us that we are "more than conquerors through Him that loved us." Our difficult circumstances are not the issue. The issue is that none of these things can separate us from the love of Christ. Notice this. We *already* have victory "in Christ!"

Someone might ask, "How can we be more than *conquerors?*" Well, think about what a conqueror has to do. A conqueror has to take personal risks, fight the battles, and plan the strategy to defeat his enemy; then, once he overcomes, the title of *conqueror* is bestowed. Paul tells us that we are *more than conquerors* because we do not have to do anything. We already have the victory. Christ is the Conqueror and we are more than conquerors. Why? Because, for us, Christ has already done it all.

We may experience some of the horrible things that Paul mentions here. However, none of them will have any bearing on our position "in Christ." That is the point. Paul closes with verses 38–39:

38 **For I am persuaded, that neither death, nor life, nor angels, nor principalities, nor powers, nor things present, nor things to come, 39 Nor height, nor depth, nor any other creature, shall be able to separate us from the love of God, which is in Christ Jesus our Lord.**

We must never forget that our Apostle Paul met the risen Lord Jesus Christ face to face. He received this revelation directly from Him. As Paul completes Romans 8, he is fully persuaded of this fact. There is absolutely nothing, past, present or future; there is no entity or power, no position or creature that can separate us from the love of God. Why is that? It is because those who are saved by grace through faith alone have been placed by the Spirit safely "in Christ!"

# Other GraceWord Publications

**In English:**

1st Corinthians: Dispensationally Considered
1st & 2nd Thessalonians: Disp. Considered
1st & 2nd Timothy & Titus: Disp. Considered
2nd Corinthians: Dispensationally Considered
Acts: Dispensationally Considered
Colossians & Philemon: Disp. Considered
Ephesians: Dispensationally Considered
Galatians: Dispensationally Considered
Hebrews: Dispensationally Considered
How Am I Wired?
Letters To Theophilus
Philippians: Dispensationally Considered
Romans: Dispensationally Considered
The Glorious Destiny Of Israel
The Gospel of John: Disp. Considered
The Gospel of Luke: Disp. Considered
The Gospel of Mark: Disp. Considered

The Gospel of Matthew: Disp. Considered
The Hidden Gospel: Once Hidden But Now Reveal.
The Seven Hebrew Epistles: Disp. Considered
Two Distinct Gospel Messages Of The N.T.

**En español:**

Cartas A Teófilo
Efesios: Dispensacionalmente considerado
El evangelio Oculto: Una vez fue un misterio

# About The Author

Steve Tackett and his wife Stephanie Tackett have been involved with the Grace Ministry for many years. Steve is well-known as a teacher, conference speaker, pastor, and evangelist. At the time of publication, he is president of Grace Bible Network which produces weekly broadcasts. They also offer online Bibles classes where people from all over the country interact with teachers. Their website is located at: www.gracebiblenetwork.org.

Steve's passion is teaching the Word of God rightly-divided. He has a uniquely adaptive teaching style which allows beginner students as well as seasoned Grace Believers to learn, understand, and enjoy their Bible. His approach places the Bible in its rightful place of authority using Scripture to teach Scripture.

www.ingramcontent.com/pod-product-compliance
Lightning Source LLC
Chambersburg PA
CBHW071707120626
46550CB00001B/140